The Byker

MARK JAMES

authorHOUSE®

AuthorHouse™ UK Ltd.
500 Avebury Boulevard
Central Milton Keynes, MK9 2BE
www.authorhouse.co.uk
Phone: 08001974150

First published by AuthorHouse 9/13/2010

ISBN: 978-1-4520-0831-8 (sc)
ISBN: 978-1-4520-0832-5 (hc)

FOREWORD

....

▣ Me!!!...I don't even pretend to be a writer. I'm pretty limited and don't have the right words. I'm broad Geordie and mostly write the way I talk...and I'm owa thick in the head to change. Even so, if I say so me-self, I can spin a good yarn.

▣ The Original **"BYKER LION"**, was the title of a little book of short stories which sold for a children's charity. Several of the tales were broadcast on local radio and resulted in an appearance on breakfast TV, being interviewed by the fabulous Lorraine Kelly.

▣ **"ME BOGIE"**, won the first prize in The Sid Chaplin Short Story Competition, in 1988.

▣ **"THE LAST NAVVY"**, also won The Sid Chaplin Short Story Competition in 2000.

▣ **"ME BOGIE, WOR WAR AND HARD GRAFT"** have all been performed on stage by an acting group of children from Local Schools.

PART ONE

> ▣ **THE BYKER LION** is a collection of short stories, most of them based on real events, only the names have been changed.

PART TWO

> ▣ **THE LAST NAVVY** stories are generally true, I've still got the lumps bumps and scars to prove it. Well apart from Murphy's Miracle which apart from the ring of stones is pure fantasy...well almost.

PART THREE

> ▣ **AND THE BLOSSOM FELL** is just good old fashioned story telling, with a few factual characters and events applied..... purely for artistic purposes.

Finally, I'd like to say how lucky I am to have been born at that time and place.

And if I had my life to live over again I can honestly say with hand on heart, that I wouldn't change a thing... not a single thing.
I'm a lucky fella and wouldn't want to be anybody else...would I....Well not now I don't!!

Mark James

DEDICATION

....

◼ I wish to dedicate this book to a very dear friend....

The Late Great

TOM HADAWAY

I would like to think a little bit of Tom's magic
rubbed off on me.

ACKNOWLEDGEMENTS

....

- I would like to thank :-

- Heaton Adult Education Centre – For giving me that second chance and showing me the way.

- My Son Shaun for his endless encouragement and assistance.

- Also Wor Lass Anthea – For just being there...and putting up with me.

Mark James

Contents

▣ *PART ONE*

The Byker Lion

Too Old For Tears

(Me and Wor Mick 1954)

By Mark James

"TOO OWLD FOR TEARS."

▣ Before I walked through the gates I made sure no one was lookin'......& I hurries' across the schoolyard.

Ashamed, whey aye I was....................me an owld fella gannin' back to school. When I knock on the classroom door, the fear was in me, all the bad memories came floodin' back...............

The times table was a complete mystery to me –

"One seven is seven...
Two sevens is....mmmmm"

I'd mumble along in tune, but never did learn the words. I couldn't spell to save me life and me worst nightmare.....my turn to get up and read out loud in front of the class.

Everybody would laugh as I tried to get me tongue around the elusive words.............

....

▣ "Come in." said a posh voice from behind the bottle Green door. With a heavy heart I turned the polished brass door knob.

"Too late for me Pet,
I'm owa thick in the head."

I told the slip of a lass. She laughed out loud and thought I was joking. I laughed along and pretended that I was.

We were encouraged to write short stories to improve our spelling. The pen was awkward to hold and the blank sheet of paper as blank as me mind. In a childish scrawl, I wrote my name. I couldn't spell February, so I didn't bother with the date.
Slowly I began to write, picking up momentum. Me spelling was terrible,

no capital letters, commas or full stops. I wrote in the way I talked, without thinking.

Long forgotten memories and voices from the past came flooding back..........................

■ I came into the world in 1939. Me motha's fourth bairn, she'd have another four.

There was a little bit of a mix up at the birth. Before me Motha even had time to say –

"Eeee warra bonny Bairn!"

In less than a heart beat, the beautiful Baby Girl was cruelly snatched away from her. In her place they plonked me. Poor Ma. she got the fright of her life.

"It's bloody horrible" She cried...
"Aa divin't want it...take it away."

She told them, before firing her new bundle of joy...like a cannon ball, into the bedside cot. Who can blame her, she'd lost an Angel and gained a gargoyle of a son. Me Fatha, a man who never pulled any punches... rubbed it in.

"Aa'll tell yer something for nowt
wor Jenny. He's nowt to look at.
By the looks of 'im, the Midwife didn't
Just smack his arse, she gave
'im a bloody good hidin'!"

..."But can yer believe it,
the little bugga's laughin' Ee's
Head off!!"

Me Ma said...."It's ownly wind, Ee's owa young too laugh...."

◾ Oh no I wasn't. Ma, God rest her soul, breast fed me in the air raid shelter while owld Hitler dropped his bombs. Old Byker then was row after row of tumble down, back-to-back soot blackened houses on the banks of the Tyne. Belchin' chimneys were our Skyline, our playgrounds – Cobbled Lanes. On bombsites we played at being Soldiers, killing each other for fun. To us, the War was only a game.

Hobnail boots clattered off slate pavements sent sparks flying as we run for the sake of running, gas-lit shadows chasing shadows.

Clammin' with the hunger and the pain of empty belly's.....a siren of Mother's voices called us safely back home.

Scrubbed clean and shining. We'd slurp down scalding hot cocoa and wolf down a door-step of Jam 'n' bread.

We had nowt.....yet we wanted for nowt, 'cause we knew no other.

All in one bed...head to toe..like sardines in a tin.
We would sleep the sleep of the dead.

....

◾ An ancient pair of blood stained boxing gloves hung from a rusty nail behind our coal house door. The blood on them was mine.

"Aa'll knock some bloody sense into yer...."

Da, promised with a snarl....then proceeded to knock out the little bit of brain I had.

"Aa'll make a bloody man of yer.."

His logic was to bray the boy outa me. I used to cry at first.....but learned to grin and bear it.

4

In time I grew bigger and stronger than the owld fella and could have murdered the owld bugga. I never did and I'm glad I didn't. He was me Fatha, yer cannit hurt yer Da'. I'd like to think I made him proud, the day he saw me bash the School bully on Byker Park...........

....

- ☐ Left School hardly able to read or write and hid the fact by going straight into a life of hard graft. Mind you, I loved bloody work, the harder the better.

Felt like I had to prove meself. I suppose I was mad at the World. Naw!, it was meself that I was mad at. Me being illiterate was a heavy cross to bear. It's a hard world, and there's always some awkward bugga who'd try an' nail me to that cross.................if I was soft enough to let 'em.

....

- ☐ I've laid bricks, stone, tarmac and concrete all on bonus. But, the hardest by far was some 18 years I spent as a Navvy, digging mile after mile of trench, laying the cables underground...............on bonus, paid by the yard.

The work would kill a bloody Horse, we all knew that, but it was all we were cut out for. Workin', drinkin', lovin' and fightin'. Thick headed Navvies, all gone but never forgotten..........a great bunch of boys. Could cry, but am too Owld for tears. I'm the only one alive an' kickin', makes yer think!.....i'm a dyin' breed.

....

- ☐ So you can imagine how I felt when for the first time in my life I signed on the dreaded dole.

I felt ashamed, when I asked the girl to fill in me form and she gave me a look that said I wasn't right in the head. By Christ I was hard to live with, being idle, nearly drove me up the wall. Too much time to think, done me head in. Wor Lass was as good as gold. It was Her who talked me into getting' meself along to an Education Centre. I joked, "I'd rather fight King Kong." But I wasn't really jokin', but when the Gran Bairn asked me to read her a bedtime story, the joke was on me.

▣   Next day I take a slow walk to the Education Centre.

I write without thinking, drifting on a mental tide into the past. Memories and voices come flooding back. Oh aye, I enjoy it but it's only a bit of fun, cannit take it owa' serious. It won't last....Why? Well it stands to reason man. The writing will definately stop, when those voices in me head run outa words. That's when I'll have nowt more to say...................................
..........hold on a minute................'til I get this little Gem down –

"What's that yer say Ma?"

....."Didn't Aa say that all 'em
Cracks on Your heed would send
Yer bloody well daft!!!"

"Aye Ma, cannit argue with that."

.....Me, Had a hard life...Nah....................................not really.

. . . .

The hardest part was picking up the pen.
Then the words came so easy.
It was as if everything I'd said and done,
all those feelings I'd ever felt.
All my dreams, the memories and more
had been locked away,
Waiting in line
just biding their time.
The pen was the key.
It unlocked the door..............................

The End

Me Bogey

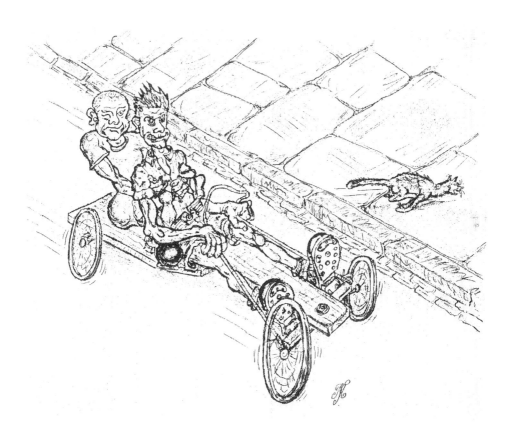

By Mark James

"Me Bogey."

By

Mark James

....

Location --   **Byker in 1950's**
Cobbled back lanes, back to back tumbledown
terraced houses.

Characters –

Marky 13 years old

Mad Mick 15 years old (Carrot Ginger)

Brian 10 years old (Markys younger brother)

Ma Late 50's (Mother of the Brothers)

Spuggy 13 years old (Markys Best mate)

Whitey 14 years old

Old Fella late 60's

Act 1 –
SCENE – BACK YARD OF AN OLD TERRACED HOUSE –
BYKER

Voice Over – Now me Motha, god bless her, already had eight kids, an' if me Fatha had got his own way,....she was going to have at least nine or ten. So, I suppose getting rid of that battered old pram was her way of saying enough was enough.
Even so, I couldn't believe me ears when she said...

Ma – "Wor Marky, gan' on and take that owld pram and dump it on Byker Quarry!!.... and mind you hurry yourself' up, before that drunken owld bugga comes in!!"

Voice Over – Now me Fatha, he was a hard man...but when me Motha Had made her mind up, there was no gannin' back.

**(We see Marky in the back yard, with pram, wheeling it backwards and
forwards. He looked spellbound at the wheels.
He's starting to work on the pram.)**

Voice Over – It was an awkward job alright...getting them wheels off without bending the axles.

Marky – Yells as he pulls the wheel... "Owww-CCHH!!!"

(We see Marky still working on the pram.)

Voice Over – I nearly gave me'self a big goolie. I just about had them off when me Motha popped her head out of the little scullery window...she didn't look owa happy.

Ma – FULL OF HELL –" And what do you want them for...ya wooden heeded bugga?"

Marky – "T'er build me bogey....Ma!!"

10

Ma – SHOUTING –" Didn't I just tell yer t' take the bugga to the tip!!"

Marky – PLEADING –" Aaahh.....But Ma, I've never had a bogey before....please Ma!"

Ma – Pausing –" Oh all reet then...gan on, but you'd better hurry yourself up or I'll come doon there and put me foot up yer backside."

Voice Over – She's got a lovely way with words, me Old Ma has!! Later on in the day I sat on me old cracket, with me elbows on me knees and me chin in me hand....staring at those lovely big wheels and dreaming of me bogey.

....

Act 2 –
SCENE – MARKY WORKING ON BOGEY.

Voice Over – It took me about a week to make. All the old bent nails had to be straightened first...before I even started.
A hole had to be burnt through the front end with a red hot poker, this would take the nut and bolt that made the front wheels swivel for the steering.
Me old saw was blunt as well as rusty...and the hammer head kept coming off.
Well, I cursed and swore every time I hit me thumb.
I called that old saw worse than muck especially...

(We see Marky jump up...holding a bloodied finger.)

......when it slipped nearly taking me finger off.
Had to suck it for ages....I didn't want me Ma to see my blood!!
I could never tell me motha when I hurt me-self....She'd kill me stone dead. Her idea of first aid was a good clout around the lug....mind you, it soon made you forget what was hurting in the first place.

**(We see finished bogey...Mark stands proud.
Spuggy and Whitey enter yard....Brian comes out back to door.)**

11

Marky – EXCITED – "Well what do you think of it???.....Gan on, tell us!!"

Spuggy – WIDE EYED – "Marky man...it's bloody great!!"

Whitey – "I've seen nowt like it!!"

Brian – "Can I have first go??"

....

Act 3 –
SCENE – MARKY SITTING OUTSIDE ON THE BOGEY

Voice Over – I was sitting there on me bogey, day dreaming...minding me own business, when who should come along and spoil me bit of peace, but Mad Mick McGinty.

(Mick enters scene.)

Voice Over – Mick was a couple of years older than me...long and skinny with carrot ginger hair.
He was famous for all the daft antics he got up to!! well he didn't get his nick-name for nowt....he was daft as a brush...The barmiest kid in Byker. He had a mouth like a thick rubber band...it scarcely parted when he spoke. The years he had spent in borstal had taught him how to speak like a ventriloquist...
He uttered his words in the same tone as his hero...Jimmy Cagney.

Mad Mick – Without moving his lips –" You've got a canny Bogey there Kidda!!"

(Mark ignores him.)

Mad Mick – LOUDER – "Are yee deef or daft...I'm not talking to me arse!!"
Voice Over – Marky still ignores him.....
.......He was trying to draw me in....but I was having none of it!!

(Marky sits on his bogey whistling to himself....as if Mick is invisible.

Mick, both hands pushed hard and deep into his pockets...his braces almost stretched to breaking point).

Mick twisted his face up, trying to look tough....An' he was making a canny job of it in' all.

Mad Mick – NICELY – "Did you make it yourself?"

Voice Over – I still said nowt.

(Micky's brow knots and he rubs his chin...then playfully kicks the bogey's front wheel.)

Mad Mick – EVEN NICER – "Big wheels them like!!"

Voice Over – He was waiting for me to bite....and I did.

Marky – PROUDLY – "Oh aye, they come off a posh pram...they did!!"

Mad Mick – SARCASTICALLY – "Hadaway t' Hell.." (Laughing)... ...."There's nee posh prams in Byker man!!"

Marky – FULL OF HELL – " Whey man...it came from Heaton (matter of factly)...didn't it (Proudly). And the wife only had one bairn an' all.... Good as new before me motha got her hands on it."

Mad Mick – SHAKING HIS HEAD IN DISBELIEF – "Never in the world....well can you believe that....only one bairn!!"

Voice Over – A devilish twinkle came into his eye...he knew I was hooked and he said...

Mad Mick – NODDING TO THE BOGEY – "I bet it could gan a bit if only we could find the right type of hill."

Voice Over – Waiting for me to fall for it....and I did.

Marky – "And what do you mean??...the right type of hill. All hills are the same....well aren't they??"

Mad Mick – SARCASTIC -- ...Laughs loudly. – "Ha!!...divent yee talk daft man!!"

Marky – PRIDE HURT – "Oh aye...and who are yee calling daft?? You're as bright as a dark night!!"

Mad Mick – FULL OF HIMSELF – "Will you shut up a minute and listen and you might just learn something for a change."

Mark – HUFFILY – "Huh!!!....me learn summit from a wooden heeded bugga like yee....Ha, that'll be the day."

Voice Over – I divent think he liked that, in fact he looked slightly vexed. His face went red and he started to growl....
....Mad Mick was definitely getting mad alright, speaking through clenched teeth he snarled...

Mad Mick – LOUDLY – "If you don't shut your hole, I'll put me fist reet in it!"

Voice Over – Even I couldn't argue that that...I bit me tongue.

Mad Mick – CALMING DOWN – "Now then, I was trying to tell you.... was the banks in Byker are all cobbles....well aren't they???"

(Marky nods...agreeing....Mick looks chuffed)
Mad Mick – CONTINUES – "Have you ever heard of tarmac??"

Marky – RESPONDING QUICKLY – "There's nee tarmac in Byker!!!"

Voice Over – A strange look came over Mick's ugly mug...and he rubbed his big dirty hands together.

Mad Mick – CONFIDENTLY – "I know a bank in Walker....just as smooth as a baby's bum."

Marky – WIDE EYED – "Tarmac!!!!!"

Mad Mick – "Aye Tarmac!!!" – (He Hacks and spits on the cobbled lane)

....

Act 4 –
SCENE – A BANK IN WALKER – MAD MICK, MARKY and BRIAN – NEAR A CHIP SHOP.

Voice Over – We sat on the bogey...looking down the steepest bank in Walker.

Marky – SCARED – "Are you sure you've been down this hill??"

Mad Mick – GRINNING WICKEDLY – "Whey aye man...I've been doon the bugga backwards."

Voice Over – Mad Mick was too daft to be scared...and me...well I was scared enough for us both!!
The smell of the fish and chip shop made me stomach growl.
A toothless old fella came out, eating a bag of chips, I would have laughed at the rubbery faces he was pulling...but not tonight.
He took one look at the two of us sitting there, ready for the off.
Pulling his face as only the toothless can...he shook his head.
Owld Fella – MUTTERING – "Bloody draft bugga's!!"

Voice Over – Mad Mick looked up at the owld man and said through clenched teeth....in his Jimmy Cagney voice....

Mad Mick – "You dirty rat you....(Cocks his finger like an imaginary gun and closes one eye.....taking careful aim.)...
.... "Pow...Pow!!!!" ....(Shooting the Owld Fella in the head.)

(The Owld Fella goes' on his way, still eating his chips.)

Owld Fella – SHAKING HIS HEAD – "Bloody daft sods!!"

Voice Over – Mad Mick said he knew every bump in the road, so we thought it best he should steer.

That made sense, but Mick was a right liar...he'd say owt but his prayers. When he started giggling to himself, doubts began to nag at the back of my mind....I hope the bogey doesn't come apart....then I shook meself... get a'had of yerself man!!!....I said to meself and even forced a sickly grin.

Brian – Hands on Marky's shoulders – "Are yer ready Wor Marky??"

....

Voice Over – Wor Brian's voice pulled me out of me trance.

I daren't let him see I was scared.

Putting on a brave face, I turned and nodded to Wor young'un.

Me heart pounded in me ears....and I had an awful pain in me belly...A voice yelled!!!!

Marky – In a dream like trance – "NOW!!!!...Wor Brian...."

(Brian pushes Marky and the Bogey.)

Voice Over -- ....and I'm certain it was mine, but I could never say for sure...

I felt Wor Brian's hands ram into the small of me back and he broke into a run.

(We see the lads bob up and down....Shakily!!!)

Voice Over -- ....The bogey shot forward and away we went.

(The Bogey Starts on its way.)

Voice Over – Mad Mick sat at the front...with his big feet placed on the wood batten fixed to the steering axle.

His long skinny body arched back like a swans neck....the rope taut in his hands.

Hanging on with me arms around his waist, I looked over his shoulder as we picked up speed...leaving the brow of the hill in our wake...

Faster and faster the wheels went bump..bump..bump across the ridges of tar. The pain in me belly escaped......by way of me arse.

(Marky Breaks wind....Mad Mick laughs loudly)

Voice Over – That made Mick laugh even louder...he was lapping it all up he was.
As the speed became frightening, fear nagged at me brain....
Suppose the bolt that held the steering snapped!!!

(We see the fear on Markys' face....and Mad grin on Mickys')

...What if we can't stop at the bottom of the hill????
I'm sure this mad bugga was trying to kill himself...and can you believe it
....here was me keeping him company.
Cursing him....I hung on for me life!!!!

Marky – YELLING – "Yoooouuuu – Bloooddy – Lunatic .... YEEEEEE!!!!"

Voice Over – Out of the corner of me eye I could see the blurred faces of on-lookers as we flashed past...
As we thundered down the bank at break neck speed....on and on...Faster and faster....the fear turned to excitement.
Mad Mick laughed a wicked laugh and let out a great big shriek.

Mad Mick – "Haaaa...Haa....Yippeeee!!!!.................Whoopeee!!!!!"

Voice Over – I joined in.

Marky – "Yipppeeee....eye....Ohhhhh!!!!"

Voice Over – And a few choice swear words' were thrown in an'all....
(Pause....) ....Waiting for us at the bottom of the hill was a hair-pin bend.
We never had a snowball in hell's chance of making it around that bend.

Marky – FEAR IN HIS VOICE – "Aaaaa....want me MMMMAAAA!!!!"

Voice Over – The front wheels ripped clean off....the axles and all.

(We see the wheels come off)

Voice Over – Them going one way....us the other...the bogey took off.

(We see the Bogey flip nose up and turn over in mid air.)

Voice Over – Sending us somersaulting through the air.

**(We see the lads rolling over a few times....and seeming to bounce off the
road....At the same moment, we see the bogey shattering as it hits the
ground...)**

Marky – Yelling – "AAAAAaaaaarrrrgggggghhhhh!!!!!"

Voice Over – I saw a flash of fire...me head exploded...I felt nowt after that.
Still going forward at great speed...we were thrown over the tarmac...all arms and legs....like a couple of rag dolls.

**(We see the lads lying flat on their backs. A few seconds of groaning and
Mad Mick staggers to his feet....Marky was flat out.)**

Voice Over – The sky pulsed...then the life left me......Body.

(We see Marky...starting to come round.)

Voice Over -- .....When I opened me eye's....I wished I hadn't.

....

Act 5 –
SCENE -- MAD MICK STANDING OVER MARKY....IN THE REMAINS OF A COMPOST HEAP. TORN PANTS AND VARIOUS SCRATCHES WITH A BLOODY NOSE.

Voice Over – Every part of me body hurt.
The abrasions on what was left of me skin burned like hot tar.

Bringing tears to me eye's and me nose dripped blood.
I lay in the remains of a muck heap....Mick's ugly mug looked down on me.

Mad Mick -- Full of concern – "Are you al'reet Kidda??....For a minute there I thought yee were dead....lucky yer landed on yer head."

Marky – Trying to un-tangle himself – "And do I look al'reet....you.....you wooden heeded bugga!!"

Mad Mick – With a feeble grin – "Now there's nee need to get nasty!!"

Marky – Full of Hell – "Nasty...Huh!!.....If I had the strength to get out of this rotten horse-dung..
I'd bloody well strangle you with me bare hands...you dirty rotten swine!!"

(We see Marky getting up...Looking a bit dazed.)

Voice Over – I staggered to me feet...more dead than alive.
The arse of me pants were ripped and I had big lumps that were getting bigger by the second.
Blood dripped from too many cuts to count....and not only that, I had left half me skin on the tarmac.
Tomorrow, I'd be one big scab.

(A Pause....)

Voice Over .... Continues -- Christ, me Ma will kill me when I get h'yem.
When I had a good look at poor old Mick....well I soon forgot about me own pain. He was like a butchers shop....and his knee cap was just about hanging off!!!!.....And there was him worrying about me.
A bit of an un-sung hero was wor Mad Mick.
I chewed on the edge of me shirt tail to weaken the cloth.
Then with a sharp flick of the wrist, it ripped straight off.
I tied it tentatively around Mick's gammy, bloodied leg.
We scrambled...bruised and battered through what was left of the fence...moaning and groaning at the effort.
As we helped each other, I knew things would never be the same...for now

there was a bond between us....Well, we were both lucky and glad to be alive...but we only half believed it.

We left that place good pals....With him calling me Marky and me calling him Micky.

Marky – WITH FEELING – "Are you sure yer al'reet there Mick Lad??'

Micky – REPLIES WITH FEELING – "Oh why'eye man...
....A'm just Champion Marky, Never felt better....and how's yersel' ...??"
Marky – "Am just as reet as rain Micky Lad...just as reet as rain!!"

Voice Over – With me arm around his waist and his arm slung over me shoulder...in a drunken walk we staggered back up the bank. I said into Micks bloodied ear....

Marky – DREAMILY – "Micky Lad...tell the truth now???...have yee ever been doon that bank before today??"

**(We See Mad Mick cough then spit and start to chuckle...
At the same time as the voice over continues...)**

Voice Over – He coughed....spat on the road and made a face....then started to chuckle before he spoke.

Mad Mick – GRINNING – "I cannot tell a lie!!!"

Marky – LAUGHING – "Are you turning over a new leaf??"

Mad Mick – Thinking Hard and grimacing – "Like I say's, the truth is I've been doon many times!!"....
(Laughs out loud) – "But never on a bogey and neither has anyone else!!"

Marky – Proudly – " So....yer reckon we're the first then??"

Mad Mick – Nodding – "Oh....aye!!!...we definitely are the first alreet!!"

Marky – Frowning -- "What makes yer so sure??"

Mad Mick – Oh aye, I'm certain....(Looks at Marky...Nodding his head.)

..."Think about it man, Marky me old mate!!"

Marky – Thinking Hard – "Mmmmm...."

Micky – "Well man, there's nee bugga daft enough to try and gan doon that hill on a bogey....now is there Marky Lad??"

(We See Marky grins a painful lopsided grin....shakes his head in agreement and laughs out loud...He hacks and spits on to the tarmac.)

(We see – the lads ambling on their way...arms around each others shoulders.)

Voice Over – We both began to laugh at the same time...and though it hurt...we laughed all the way home.
Folk's passing us on the way nodded their heads and muttered...
...................."Bloody Daft Bugga's!!"

(We See – The Lads in the distance...limping on their way...still laughing.)

Voice Over – Bloody?...Aye, we certainly were....
........Daft???
Well there's nee arguing with that!!!!!

....

THE END

"The Bogey shot forward...
...and away we went!"

The Byker Lion

By Mark James

Place:--   *Byker – working class.*

Time:--   *Early '50s*

We see:--   *Back to back, tumbled down houses, gas lamps & belching* *chimneys.*

We hear:-- *'Green and pleasant land – Jerusalem'*

We see a boy's school Gym. A class of 14 year olds dressed in P.T. kit, baggy shorts & sandshoes, stand in line at attention, ready for inspection.

V.O.

It was like an ice-factory in that gym, and we had t' stand there just in shorts. Mine were four sizes owa' big. Me feet were blue with the cold, sandshoes were a luxury me Motha' couldn't afford. When in he walks, Mr bloody Wonderful, Mr Hearty, our new P.T. Teacher *(we see a Greek God of a man)*. Aa didn't like the fella the first time Aa set eyes on him, Aa don't think he thought too much of us either, mind yer! He stood there posin', hands on hips, broad-shouldered and sun-tanned, the perfect all-round Athlete, looking down on us with contempt – the big-headed, arrogant bugger!!!

Aa could tell by the look on his face he didn't want t' be there, in fact Aa'm sure he wasn't, not in mind anyhow, he seemed miles away! *(we see a close-up of Mr Hearty's face, daydreaming, countryside, sunshine, to the music of 'Grieg's Morning')*

Mr Hearty had just arrived that mornin', he was still in a state of shock at the culture change standin' before him, after all, he'd come from one of the posh schools in High Heaton *(we see the school, a beautiful stone building, with trees, flowerbeds and vast playing fields with Rugby posts)*. Yer know the kind of school Aa mean, where they wore uniforms with fancy badges on the pockets an' them daft little caps *(we see the 'posh' kids, dressed immaculate)*, where the kids want for nowt and play Rugby *(we see a Rugby match in progress, all the players clean-cut and well turned out)*, because they're no good at the real game, Football! *(we see a bunch of kids, strips too big, baggy shorts, covered in mud, chasing a football, shouting and swearing).* Aa suppose it must have been a bit of a shock to his privileged system, ha, he stood there like an Angel who'd just lost his wings *(we see Mr Hearty blink both eyes as he wakens from his dream, his eyes widen as he scans the class, the music suddenly changes to 'Carmina Burana', The Omen theme).* Before him stand 4B, the scruffiest class in the scruffiest school in the East end! His eyes swept over each sorry lookin' specimen in turn, searchin' for the worst individual of a bad bunch to exact his revenge on for his own recent misfortunate career tumble, *(the music stops abruptly)* they stopped and stared at me!

MR. HEARTY *(Sgt. Majorish)*:

What's your name boy? And speak up!!!

MARKY *(sheepish):* J...James.

MR. HEARTY: James, James what?

MARKY *(hand shooting up in air)*:

The Steam Engine!

MR. HEARTY *(nasty look):*

You trying to be funny boy??? 'Sir' is the word I'm looking for!!!

MARKY *(innocent):* Naw Sir, James Watt, Sir, he invented the steam engine, Sir, but Geordie Stephenson invented the steam train, sir, The Rocket!

MR. HEARTY *(with contempt):*
What on Earth are you on about, boy? *(pause)* We'll try again, shall we, what is your name, boy???

25

MARKY: James.

MR. HEARTY (*Sgt. Major shout*):

              James, SIR!!!

MARKY (*sticking chest out*):

              James, Sir!!!, Sir.

MR. HEARTY (*condescending*):

              James, boy (*looking down at feet*), where's your
              gym shoes?

MARKY (*almost a whisper*):

              Aa haven't got any, Sir.

MR. HEARTY (*smirking, with raised voice*):

              Speak up boy, I didn't quite catch that, you
              what?

MARKY (*embarrassed, with slightly raised voice*):

              Aa...Aa haven't got any sandshoes, SIR!!!

V.O.

Aa said, tryin' t' hide me dirty feet at the same time, by curlin' up me toes,
like a Budgie on a perch. But there was no foolin' this fella', he was like a
Dog with a bone, me bein' the bone! (*Mr Hearty leant over and yelled in
Marky's ear*).

MR. HEARTY: Just look at the colour of your feet, boy!!!

Fearing the worst, Aa glanced down, (*we see a close up of a pair of dirty feet with curled up toes)* Aa had taken the short-cut over Shell-shocked Sams' allotment, it had been awful wet. The clarts had squelched up through the holes in me boots. Me cotton socks had went stiff, and the mud had hardened between me toes. *(we see the scenes)*

In the changin' room, Aa'd gouged most of it out, before spittin' on me shirt tail, Aa rubbed me feet, like me Motha' would rub the Donkey-stone on the doorstep, but it was no good, Aa had run out of spit and time. So bravely, Aa entered the gym, sand-shoeless with the remains of the baked muck, still set between me toes. What was worse, me wet feet dried the colour of mud, there was no hidin' it!

MR. HEARTY: JAMES!!!

MARKY: Aye Sir...Aa mean yes Sir.

MR. HEARTY: *(top of voice):*

You're a disgrace to the School!!!

We see Mr. Hearty grab Marky by the ear and twist it up-over, forcing Marky to stand on his tip-toes.

MARKY *(in pain, grimacing):*

A-ya, oy-ah, oy-yaaaa...

MR. HEARTY *(growling):*

What are you?

MARKY: Aa'm...Aa'm a disgrace t' the School, Sir!
We see Mr. Hearty marching Marky from the gym by the ear.

In the changing room, we see Marky, on his own. He stands on one leg, with one foot in the Wash-Basin, the tap is running.

MR. HEARTY *(from other side of door, his voice fading).*

27

And don't you dare come back until you've washed your feet good and proper, you...you scruffy little gutter-urchin, you, you're nothing but.......

MARKY   (*cursing under his breath, looks at himself in the mirror, tears in his eyes*):
Aa'll get even with yer, yer dirty rotten swine, wait an' see, one of these days!

MARKY'S REFLECTION:

Ha!!! That's a bloody laugh, look at the state of yer, yer as strong as a minty bullet, an' a half-sucked one at that!!!

MARKY   (*astonished*):
W...w...what? Who...who?

REFLECTION: Aye, ye, Aa've seen stronger perfume on yer Motha's dressin' table!

MARKY: An' who the bloody Hell d' yer think you're talkin' to, like? (*waves fist*) Aa'll give yer a fat lip in a minute!

REFLECTION: Ha, ye an' who's army? Yer couldn't punch yer way out of a wet paper bag!

MARKY: Aa'll show yer, Aa'll show 'em all! Aa will, Aa'm tellin' yer, Aa bloodywell will, just ye wait an' see!!!

V.O.

One way or another, Aa was certainly goin' to prove mesel', even if only t' mesel'! *(waves fist at reflection, as reflection waves fist back, and becomes no more than a mirror image, losing its' temporary independence, once again being controlled by Marky)*

Scene:-- Main Street in Byker. A rundown, second hand book-shop. Marky gazes dreamily in the window. We see a close up through the window, and scan the rows of books, mostly Boxing. On the cover of 'The Ring', famous fighters pose a familiar fighting stance. We stop at 'Rocky Marciano, The Brocton Blockbuster, The Heavyweight Champion of the world'.

Marky daydreams, to the music 'Nimrod'.

ROCKY *(from the cover, winks):*

> So yer wanna be a fighter, kid?

MARKY *(astonished, mouth agape, nods head):*

> Er, er, aye, sure. Aa can just see mesel', *'The Byker Blockbuster'.*

We see the name 'Rocky Marky-ano' in big, bold, red silk letters on the back of a golden boxing robe. The crowd roar as Marky-ano steps under the ropes and enters the ring. The crowd chant "Marky, Marky, Marky..." The fighters walk to the centre of the ring.

REFS' VOICE: Okay boys, I wanna good, clean fight, shake hands and come out fighting.

Marky returns to his corner, disrobes and turns to meet his opponent, trying to look tough. The Ref steps between the fighters. Marky looks up at the Refs' face, it's Mr. Hearty!

MR. HEARTY: Stop, hold on a minute. Where's your gym-shoes, boy?

The crowd laugh. Marky blushes bright red, as we see his bare, dirty feet.

MARKY *(to himself, mutters):*

> Bastard!!! *(aloud, to Mr Hearty)* Haven't got any, Sir!

The crowd roar with laughter as Mr. Hearty marches Marky from the ring and down the aisle by his ear.

We are inside the bookshop.

MARKY *(to shopkeeper):*

> Much are yer books, Mister?

SHOPKEEPER *(broken nose, cauliflower ear, ex pugilist):*

> Which one's?

MARKY *(pointing with thumb):*

> The one's in the window.

SHOPKEEPER: Yer mean Mags, all d'pends on what yer want, kid.

MARKY: 'The Ring'.

SHOPKEEPER: Ha, Boxin', bloody Mugs game that is, Son, all end up punch-drunk. Anyway, yer couldn't afford them, best stick with yer comics *(points to a pile on the counter)*, we got the lot there, Dandy, Beano, Film-fun, all a Penny each or a Ha'penny swap.

MARKY *(determined):*

Na! Aa'm too old for comics, man, Aa leaves School next year.

SHOPKEEPER: What d'yer wanna be when yer grows up, Son?

MARKY *(thinks hard, sticks chest out):*

A man!

SHOPKEEPER: Well, there's no arguin' wi' that, Aa hope yer makes it, there's a lot that don't. So yer think bein' a Boxer's gonna make yer a man, eh?

MARKY: Naw, a fighter! *(swings fists)* Aa just wanna be a fighter!

SHOPKEEPER *(laughs, and gives Marky a fun left hook with open hand to side of head):*

Don't forget t' dook, kidda, Aa didn't! Anyway, back t' business. Righto, killer, which Mags d'yer want, they're all different prices.

MARKY: Why's that?

SHOPKEEPER: Yer pays for quality, Son, now there's a valuable lesson yer've just learnt. *(points to window)* All collectors items them, some's worth a small fortune!

MARKY: Which one's them like?

SHOPKEEPER: Big names, Son, big names. Joe Louis, Sugar Ray Robinson, Jack Dempsey and the likes, now which one d'yer fancy? Name a name!

MARKY: Marciano, the one with Rocky Marciano on

the cover!

SHOPKEEPER: Rocky Marciano, the undefeated heavyweight champion of the world, yer talkin' big money there, Son.

MARKY: How big?

SHOPKEEPER *(thinks)*:

Oh, say three an' six.

MARKY *(shocked)*: Eh! Yer kiddin', aren't yer? Aa've only got a tanner, man!

SHOPKEEPER *(laughs, rubs Markys' head)*:

Son, forget about Rocky an' go an' get yersel' a stick o' rock instead, an' Aa'll let yer have two comics for the price o' one. Ye stick with Desperate Dan an' Dennis the Menace an' don't be in such a hurry t' grow up, eh!
Marky is dejected, and turns to go.

SHOPKEEPER: So long, Champ, come back when yer grown up, an' if yer still interested in the fight game, Aa'll take yer under me wing. An' by the way Son, me name's Casey, Cast-iron Casey!

MARKY *(turns, smiling)*:
W...Wha...what, who? 'The' Cast-iron Casey, the man with the iron jaw, made in the Shipyards!

SHOPKEEPER *(smiling)*:
Aye, Son, that's me, tho' Aa'm a little rusty now, but as Aa says, Aa'll show yer the ropes when yer ready!

MARKY:	Will yer, will yer really Mr. Cast-iron?
SHOPKEEPER:	Aye, certainly will, Son, but yer have a lot o' fillin' out t' do before then. If yer don't mind us askin', yer haven't been ill, have yer?
MARKY:	Who? Me, naw, why like?
SHOPKEEPER:	It's just that, well, no offence like, but yer well, er, A bit skinny an' pale as an albino's white-bits, man, yer gonna have t' build yersel' up a bit!
MARKY:	Well, how do Aa start that, eh?
SHOPKEEPER:	Exercise, Son, exercise, an' plenty of it. Had on a minute, Aa've just had a thought, have yersel' a rake through that pile of books over there in the corner. There's all sorts, Weightlifting, Bodybuilding an' all that sort of thing. Some of them's ancient mind yer, but take yer time, yer might just find summat yer want. An' just t' start yer on the right road, just for you, mind Aa wouldn't do it for anybody else, so don't yer be goin' tellin' anyone, but sayin' as yer me pal, take yer pick for a Tanner!
MARKY	*(excited):* Great! Thanks Mr. Casey!!!
SHOPKEEPER:	Oh, think nowt of it, kidda! Who knows, yer might be a Champion one o' these days, an' the road t' fame an' glory all started in old Casey's corner shop! By the way, Son, me first name's Jack, just call me Jack.
MARKY:	Pleased t' meet yer Jack, *(they shake hands)* an' thanks a lot Jack!

V.O.

The book was red, that's how it caught me eye *(we see a close up of the book, titled 'The Russian Lion'),* His name was foreign, Aa could hardly read English, never mind foreign!

We see a shabby bedroom. Pictures of Jackie Milburn and Rocky Marciano are stuck up on the wall. Marky is lying on the bed, looking at his little red book.

MARKY *(struggling to read the name on the cover):*

> Ge-or-ge, er, Ha-a-cken-sch-midt *(looks up from book)* What a bloody mouthful! *(turns over cover)* Wowww!!! Worra man!!!

V.O.

George Hackenscmidt, the Russian Lion, was the greatest Wrestler the World has ever known. When Aa turned the cover, there he was in all his glory. Aa've never been so excited in all me life, he was built like a brick wall, 21" neck, 52" chest, his arms and legs were as thick as tree-trunks. George was everything Aa wanted t' be, big strong, invincible. Aa was truly smitten. *(we see pictures in book).*

His book was goin' t' change my life, all Aa had t' do was read it. *(we see Marky reading book)* Mind yer though, that was easier said than done, readin' wasn't me strong point! Slowly and painfully Aa began. The first page was the hardest, even so, Aa was determined to read an' t' learn, slowly but steadily, Aa did. George Hackenschmidt had died ages ago, but his spirit had lain hidden away in that little red book. Just like the Genie in the bottle, just waiting there for someone t' open the cover. That certain somebody just so happened t' be me. Aa found it hard t' take in all in at first as Aa struggled over the words. So when Aa'd eventually stuttered and stammered my way through the book, Aa read it again, more slowly this time, more focussed, almost obsessed, it seemed as if, well, as if it was him tellin' me the story. The more Aa read, the realer he seemed t' become, as if the book had came t' life, or so it seemed. *(we see picture of Hackenschmidt in trunks. The picture comes to life. His muscles bulge as he goes through his posing routine)* Aa'm sure Aa became possessed with

George Hackenschmidts' ghost! Maybe Aa was dreamin', Aa don't know, all Aa know is it seemed real enough t' me, me imagination just seemed t' run away, with me in tow! *(Hackenschmidt finishes routine, winks and takes a bow).*

MARKY *(flabbergasted, rubs eyes):*

Nice one George! Aa've been dyin' t' meet yer Mr. Hackenschmidt. *(puts hand over mouth)* Err, no offence, like, didn't mean t' say dyin', hope Aa didn't hurt yer feelin's.

GEORGE: Don't worry, Son, err, by the way, what's yer name?

MARKY *(proud):* Marky, Marky James.

GEORGE: Pleased to meet you, Marky James. Just call me Geordie. *(Georges' hand comes out of the book. Marky takes hold of it. They shake)*

MARKY: My pleasure, *(frowning)* but Aa hope yer don't mind us sayin' so, yer speak awful good English, for a Russian, like.

GEORGE: Why aye, man, what d'yer expect, me Ma' came from North Shields, didn't she!

MARKY: So yer Da' was Russian, then?

GEORGE: Naw, he was a bloody Pitman from Durham!

MARKY: Well how did yer get the name Hackenschmidt?

GEORGE: Well, me real name's Woodcock, but all the kids at school took the piss, an' that's probably why Aa took up Wrestlin'. Anyway, Aa decided

35

that Aa needed a name that would catch the eye an' roll off the tongue, a name that would carry mystery and intrigue about it. Well, Aa thought there was always somethin' about foreign names, the crowds always love t' hate the foreigners, always gets them flockin' in as well. It took me ages t' find the right name, all the best ones had been taken. Anyway, it just came out of the blue one day, yer'll not believe this, but with me Fatha' bein' a Pit-yacker, he always had a phlegmy throat, an' was always hackin' an' a spittin' in t' the back of the fire *(snaps his fingers),* an' there yer have it, Hack-in-smit!!!

MARKY *(excited):*   So yer not even a little bit Russian?

GEORGE: Naw, Geordie by name an' Geordie by nature, born an' bred in Newcastle!

MARKY *(excited):*   Great, maybe Aa could do the same, but then again Aa doubt it!

GEORGE: How's that young fella'?

MARKY: Well, Aa wouldn't know what to call mesel' for starters!

GEORGE: Don't be daft, man, all yer need t' do is use yer imagination a little, an' the name'll come when yer least expectin' it. But not t' worry, there's plenty of time for that, first things first, eh, but before we start, what year would this be, young fella'?

MARKY: Er, it's 1953, why like?

GEORGE *(dreamily):*

Christ, Aa've been gone for 50 bloody years! Who's the current reignin' Heavyweight Wrestlin' Champion of the World?

MARKY *(laughing):*   Wrestlin'? Aa don't know, t' tell yer the truth, Aa don't know if there is one but Rocky Marciano's the Boxin' Champ, undefeated he is!

GEORGE: *(taken aback):*

Hmmm, Boxin', never in the world, Aa never dreamed the old fisty-cuffs would catch on. Anyway, Aa'm here for much more important business than that!

MARKY: An' what's that, like?

GEORGE *(rubbing hands together):*

Well, a difficult task it may be, bonnie lad, but Aa'm here t' make a man of your good self!

MARKY *(excited):*   What? Bloodywell great man, when do we start?

GEORGE: Well, Aa suppose now's as good a time as any. *(powerful voice)* You're going to be as brave as a Lion and as strong as a Bull.

MARKY: Who, me?

GEORGE: Yes, you!

MARKY: H...h...how? Aa'll never be as big an' strong as you!

GEORGE: First things first, young Marky, Aa'll tell yer this for starters *(points to his head)* It's all in the

	mind, inner strength, that's the key!
MARKY *(puzzled):*	An' how d' yer mean like?'
GEORGE:	Simple, a man can be anything or anybody he wants to be. Re-invent yerself in your minds eye, and you will become that invention. In other words, believe in yourself, or nobody else will believe in you!
MARKY:	Well, fair enough. Aa suppose that makes snese, 'cos me Da' always says Aa was a useless bugger an' Aa believed him.
GEORDIE:	Aye, an' when the seeds of doubt are sown at an early age, the tree of life will never grow strong. Lucky for you, it's not too late, alas, many go t' their grave none the bloody wiser.
MARKY:	Aa've heard that before, it's in the little red book, ain't it!
GEORDIE:	Hah, a fair scholar we have here, that is a positive start, good lad, but Aa bet yer can't remember the first sentence on the first page?
MARKY *(thinking):*	Erm, er, aye, got it! Page one, Chapter one, 'Self-belief', *'Aa'm goin' t' be powerful, Aa'm goin' t' be invincible, Aa'm goin' t' be brave as a Lion an' strong as a bloody Ox!'*

We hear Ma's voice shouting up the stairs.

MA:	Wor Marky, is that ye talkin' t' yersel' up there, yer barmy bugger, they'll come an' take yer away if yer not careful!
MARKY:	Me, naw Ma', Aa'm just sayin' me prayers, 'Brave as a Lion, strong as an Ox, Amen'. *(music*

to 'The Swan')

V.O.

Whatever Geordie said, Aa would do or die tryin' it. He was my hero, my mentor, for the first time in me life, Aa believed in someone, one day Aa'd be just like him, *(we see Marky posing in front of bedroom mirror),* Aa could see it all, just as plain as day, *(we see Marky daydreaming, in his dream he stands in the centre of a wrestling ring, hands above his head, the crowd cheers, to the music of 'Nimrod'. On the back of his red, silk robe in a fierce Lions' golden head, surrounded in big, gold letters, 'The Champ – The Byker Lion'. Marky disrobes, he's built like Hercules, the crowd go wild and chant his name as one, 'Byker lion – Byker Lion – Byker Lion'. Marky shows off his muscles. We hear the referee's voice, loud and clear, 'Ladies and Gentlemen, introducing to you, the undefeated Heavyweight Champion of the World, Mar-keee Jayyy-mes...' the crowd go wild, '...the one and onlyyy, BYYYY-KER LIIII-ON!!!' (Back to reality, we see Marky's in front of the bedroom mirror, striking up a wrestling pose and twisting up his face into a fighting snarl).*

MARKY *(to reflection):*

> Boy, Aa'm ain't half skinny!

V.O.

It was true, Aa looked for all the world like a skinned Rabbit, Aa could count me ribs. Aa couldn't go into the Wrestlin' ring lookin' like that, Aa'd be the laughin' stock of Byker!

MARKY *(to himself):*

> Aa could wear a mask Aa suppose, *(pulls a sock over his head, growls)* 'The Masked Marvel', naw *(pulls sock off head)*, it's been done before *(laughs)*, anyway, Aa'd look even more like a matchstick!

We see Marky ambling down a back lane, an old sack over his shoulder, (music – Peter and the Wolf)

MARKY *(yells)*: Any owld rags' an' jam jars, any owld rags an' jam jars!

V.O.

It took me two weeks collectin' rags an' jam jars to pay for me chest expanders.

We see a pair of chest expanders in a second-hand shop window. Marky goes in, the door-bell tinkles. The expanders are removed from the window. Marky comes out smiling, a brown paper parcel tucked under his arm. He walks away, the expanders dangling out the back of the parcel.

We see Marky in his bedroom, stripped to the waist, with the chest expanders.

V.O.

Aa put mesel' through seven sorts of Hell with them things, *(we see Marky struggling with expanders)*. Some of the positions Aa got mesel' into had t' be seen t' be believed, *(we see Marky straining in a number of positions with expanders)*. It was a fight between me an' them expanders, it was a fight Aa had t' win. After Aa was finished me routines, *(music Nimrod)*, Aa used t' pose in front of the mirror, just like Geordie did in the book, *(we see Marky posing)*.

MARKY *(to himself)*:

Can't see a ha'pennies worth o' difference! *(looks up to picture of Hackenschmidt on the wall)* But Aa'm not givin' up Geordie, even if it kills me, Aa'm not givin' up! *(picks up expanders and starts exercises again)*.

We see the back garden.

V.O.

We had recently moved from old Byker to this house in St. Anthony's, with a garden. Aa made this me trainin' ground. (we see Marky training, press-ups, sit-ups, squats, pull-ups, dips etc.)
On the ends of a heavy wooden pole, Aa tied bricks, (we see Marky with improvised weights), this was me barbell.

On me Motha's clothes-line hung a punch-ball, which Aa used t' knock Hell out of, (we see Marky bobbing and weaving, punching ball), Aa used t' pretend that it was me Fatha', Aa even painted his face on it, an' if Aa say so mesel', it was the double of him! Boy, Aa used t' love bashin' that ball!

However, it has t' be said that the trainin' wasn't without mishap, (we see Marky straining with chest expanders, at full stretch, red, contorted faced, tries to hold it and fails) Aa nearly choked mesel' in me chest expanders, (we see expander springs entangled around Markys neck), An' Aa nearly killed mesel' with me home-made barbell, (we see Marky, straining with barbell above head), when the pole snapped an' the bricks came together, (we see the pole snap and Marky screams in agony as the bricks come together), with me in the middle!
The word soon got round when Aa was havin' a work-out, all the windows would open and the neighbours would hang out, waiting (we see the neighbours at their windows) for the one man show t' start. If Aa could have sold tickets, Aa'd have made a small fortune. The audience had a good laugh at me antics, they had a good right t' laugh as well, (we see Marky struggling with a few of his training routines).

George Hackenschmidt ate more in a single day than Aa ate in a whole year, the greedy bugger! Aa had t' eat more, drippin' an' bread wasn't goin' t' build a body like big Georgies'. Me Fatha' was on the dole, which meant Aa was entitled t' free school meals, (we see Marky in an orgy of gluttony in school dinner hall), and now that Aa had a cause, Aa ate everything Aa could get me teeth into, includin' second helpin's and anythin' else that the fussy kids left! Aa'd even drink all the left over milk.

Finally, Aa laid me hands on a book in the local Library, about Wrestlin', (we see Marky going through various Wrestling moves in the bedroom mirror). After practising all the moves from the book, it was now the time to try them out for real. Aa was gettin' a bit sick of Wrestlin' with mesel'. Aa knew all me own moves, sometimes Aa'd almost end up in a bloody knot!

(we see the back garden) Aa fixed up a ring in the back garden with me Motha's old clothes line, (we see the ring), an' wor Brian was me first reluctant opponent, (we see Brian, worried, stripped to the waist, moving forward in a Wrestling crouch). Him bein' younger than me, he didn't really want t' Wrestle, he wanted t' play Cowboys, but Aa finally coaxed him by promisin' him the Moon, well, a lend of me catapult anyway! (we see the lads Wrestling, to the music 'Sabre Dance'), Aa was never a bully, and Aa was as gentle as Aa could be with wor kid, (we see Brian in a Half-Nelson, Bear-hug, Full-Nelson, grimacing, with a look of agony on his face), but it always ended up in tears, with wor Brian runnin' up the garden path bubblin' his eyes out, and me Motha' runnin' down t' have a go at me. Even though Aa needed bigger and stronger opponents, (we see Marky in full flight, his Mother giving chase, waving a fist), Aa don't think Aa was ready for me Motha' yet, t' tell the truth, Aa think Geordie might've ran from me Motha'!

(we see the schoolyard) At school Aa soon became a bit of a hero in the schoolyard, (we see a close up of Marky in Wrestling stance, he moves forward, we go up and over, ending up looking at the sky), Aa put bullies on their backs in seconds, bullies that had been plaguing all the quieter an' softer kids, mesel' included, for years, (we see Marky looking down on us, grinning), yep, revenge was sweet!

(in the school gym, we see the class in line) Aa still hated P.T., standin' there half-naked, freezin' with the cold, teeth chatterin', knees knockin'. But Aa was actually lookin' forward t' this lesson, Aa'd managed t' acquire mesel' a tatty pair o' black sand shoes from the lost property box, (we see Marky's feet) although they were at least two sizes over big, Aa was still proud of them!

CLASS (sings & dances):

> Dem bones, dem bones, dem dry bones, oh hear the word of the Lord. Dem bones, dem bones gonna walk around, dem bones, dem bones gonna walk around, hear the word of the Lord.

MARKY: Watch it! Here comes Mr. Supershit himself! Look at his fancy vest, man, and lily white sand-shoes.

Aa bet he thinks he looks great, but Aa reckon he looks like a right bloody puff!

Mr. Hearty swaggers over. The class comes to attention.

V.O.

My God, what a sight we looked, we looked like a line-up for Mr. Punyverse! Despite me rigorous bout of exercisin', Aa was still as skinny as a rake, an' them shorts that me Motha' got us from the Pawn shop, were four sizes over big, they made me legs look even skinnier, if that was at all physically possibe, an' the sand shoes didn't help! On cold days, the hairs on me legs would stand on end, makin' them look like hairy Caterpillars!

MR. HEARTY: Good morning, boys!
CLASS: Mornin', Sir!

MR. HEARTY (sarcastic):

What a fine bunch of manhood we have here. Britain shall never again tremble in the wake of War, (swaggers over to mat). Right boys, over here, and at the double! (the boys move over to the mat) Right, form a circle around the mat, quick, move it, c'mon, c'mon! (he scans the rabble before him) Today boys, I'm going to teach you the fundamentals of Wrestling.

V.O.

Well, Aa couldn't believe me ears!

MR. HEARTY (points a finger at pupils, sticks out his chest):

You, you and you! (his finger shot out at his three victims, me among them), White! Come over here boy!

WHITEY (pointing to himself):
Who, me Sir?

MR. HEARTY (sarcastic):

Yes you, boy, unless we have another pupil by the name of White with us! (class laughs, Whitey skulks over to mat) Right White, put your right hand around the back to my neck and your left around my lower back.

WHITEY (joking):   Aa didn't know yer cared, Sir! (class laughs)

MARKY (whispering to Smiggy):

Aa told yer he loves us all!

Smiggy uncontrollably bursts out laughing.

MR. HEARTY: You'll see the funny side of it in a minute, Smith, you're next!

Smiggy straightens up, but is struggling to keep his laugh in.

SMIGGY: S...sorry, Sir!

MR. HEARTY: You will be! Right boy, sorry to keep you waiting, now back in position, bend your knees, crouch down and tuck your head into my shoulder, right, now take the strain.

WHITEY: Don't we need music for this, Sir? (class laughs)

MARKY (sings):   Dance with me, hold me closer, closer and closer...

MR. HEARTY (still in Wrestling stance):

Don't worry James boy, I'll be saving the last dance for you! (turns his attention back to Whitey) Right now, (yells) HEAVE, up and over you go! (the class, as one, grimace in sympathy for Whitey)

V.O.

Poor Whitey, it was all over in the blink of an eye with Whitey winded, (we see Whitey flat on his back) on his back, he landed like a Ton of bricks.

MR. HEARTY (chest sticking out, full of himself):

Smith boy, over here, you seem to have lost your laugh!

V.O.

He never did like big Smiggy, (we see Smiggy look around for moral support) he was the biggest kid in the school and as strong as an Ox. Even so, Smiggy went the same way as Whitey, (we see Smiggy going up and over) up and over. It's true what they say, the bigger they are, the harder they fall, he went down like a Lancaster Bomber full of Lead, with arms outstretched with a sickening thud, (we see Smiggy hit the deck, belly first, with a loud 'OOOF', once again, a sympathetic groan from the class. Then silence, as Mr. Hearty turned to Marky and smiled evilly, to the music 'Carmina Burana', we see Marky, a look of terror on his face).

MR. HEARTY (growls):

James, I believe you have the privilege of the last dance!

At the sound of me own name, me knees nearly buckled an' me stomach churned, (we see Marky, looking shocked), he had left me 'til last, he'd wanted t' make the biggest fool out of me in front of the whole class. (we see Marky, looking around at the rest of the class for moral support) this bloke came from a different planet, a world where t' lose face was the worst thing that could happen t' yer, play the game, charge for the guns an' all that crap, no place for the loser! (we see Mr. Hearty walking back and forwards, never taking his eyes off Marky, rubbing his hands together, chest puffed out) Bloody full of himsel', he was, struttin' around like somebody not right in the head, and by Christ, he was lovin' every minute of it!

MR. HEARTY (approaches Marky, screams aggressively in his face, spraying every word):

> JAMES!!! Are you deaf boy, or just a bleeding coward?

V.O.

Aa couldn't speak, Aa couldn't move, (we see Marky, frozen) Aa just stood there rooted t' the spot. Aa was almost ready t' turn an' run when Aa heard a familiar voice.

GEORGE:	The moment of truth has arrived, Marky Lad, your fate is now in your own hands, go for it and be brave, Byker Lion.
	We see a vision of George, addressing Marky, Teacher to the pupil, who steps back, astonished.
MARKY:	B...b...but...
GEORGE:	But what, lad?
MARKY:	But, but Aa'm scared, Geordie, scared shitless. Aa gone an' tried me best, Aa did, honest t' God, Aa really did!
GEORGE:	Be positive, Marky Son, yer've got t' believe in yersel', remember, have self-belief!
MARKY:	What? Believe in mesel', Aa've tried me best Geordie, but Aa've bee kiddin' mesel' all along, throwin' me little Brother around in the garden an' then a few kids' in the school yard, thinkin'

GEORGE:	Aa was a bloody Wrestler, it's all been a load of shit, man, Aa'm not a Wrestler, never will be! But yer can be a Wrestler, Son, like Aa told yer, yer can be anybody yer bloodywell like, it's all in the mind!
MARKY:	Hah, that's easy for you t' say, but it doesn't make any sense t' me, yer can only be yersel' at the end of the day, can't yer!
GEORGE:	Right, now listen carefully, Son, think hard now. Who would yer really like t' be at this moment in time?
MARKY:	Well, er, Aa suppose Aa'd wanna be you!
GEORGE:	Well then, focus yer mind and be me!
MARKY:	What, but how?
GEORGE:	Well, yer already are me, Marky lad, yer ever heard of reincarnation?
MARKY:	Aye, that tinned milk stuff, what about it?
GEORGE (laughs):	Naw, stupid! Listen, we all have a soul, right, yer with me?
MARKY:	Aye, like heart an' soul, Aa know what yer mean, but what're yer tryin' t' say?
GEORGE:	What Aa'm sayin' is the soul is immortal, the body dies, but the soul lives on, it's just reborn into another body, and in your case, my soul has been reincarnated into your body.
MARKY:	Get away t' Hell, yer havin' us on!

GEORGE:	Naw, let's think, how can Aa put it, like waves, aye, that's it, just like waves, one dies, either crashing against the rocks, or gently ripplin' onto the shore, then the soul leaves the dead wave and immediately enters another wave, which is formed miles out t' sea, reborn in the middle of the ocean, beginnin' it's inevitable journey back t' the shore, t' once again die an' start the whole lifecycle all over again!
MARKY:	Well, that sort of makes sense, but you died bloody far too long ago for your soul t' pop into me when Aa was born!
GEORGE:	Aye, true enough, bonnie lad, but my soul has been in limbo, all these years Aa've been floatin' around, searchin', waitin' for the right host t' come along.
MARKY:	What, yer mean like the Genie in the bottle?
GEORGE:	Aye, exactly like that, just like waitin' for a new Master.
MARKY:	Aa've got it! The book, when Aa opened the book, whoosh, out yer came. Aa remember this funny feelin' at the time, like, like tingly all over. (thinks hard) But hold on a mo', why did yer wait so long t' put us in the picture? Could have saved us a load of bother tellin' us earlier!
GEORGE:	Simple, yer had t' prove yersel' first, Marky lad!
MARKY:	An' did Aa?
GEORGE:	Yer certainly did that, my boy, now Aa must be on me way, my task is done, an' your fate is now yours t' control, so good luck an' always believe in yersel', Marky lad! (pause, as they both nod at

each other appreciatively) An' by the way Son, take those stupid bloody things off yer feet, they're a liability, they are!

V.O.

Then 'Poof', he was gone, just like that! (we see George disappear in a puff of smoke, much to the amazement of Marky, who wakes out of his dream, when George is replaced by an angry Mr. Hearty)

MR. HEARTY (screaming, red in the face):

JAMES BOY, WAKE UP!!! (growling) Over here, now, and move it!

V.O.

A funny feelin' came over me, like Aa was possessed or something', Aa think that was the right word, (we see Marky, chest out, slips off his sand shoes, walks onto the mat, eyeing Mr. Hearty) anyways, Aa really believed George Hackenschmidt had taken over me body and soul. A different lad walked proudly over t' the mat. It went deathly silent as we stood facin' each other in the centre of the mat, an' Aa remember lookin' him in the eye an' thinkin' t' mesel', "Aa'm gonna murder this big headed, bullyin' swine!"

(we see the scene) We came t' grips, his muscular arms wrapped, 'round me back, my skinny arms 'round his. Round an' round we went, one way, then the other, almost crab-like. He tried t' dump me, but Aa was ready for him, Aa hung onto him like a limpet on a rock. Aa could feel the strength in his vice-like arms. Pullin' me one way, an' then the other as he tried t' take me off balance, but Aa moved with the tide an' kept me weight low. That failin', he tried t' lift me off me feet by pure brute force alone, but instinctively Aa countered the move, by crouchin' low, with me legs wide apart, grippin' the mat with me toes, at the same time thankin' George for the advice about discardin' me sand shoes. He wouldn't give up though. How long we stayed locked in combat, Aa don't know, all Aa know is he wouldn't give an inch, but neither would Aa.
Gruntin' an' groanin', the struggle went on, somebody had t' give. A

weakness came over me, Aa felt sick in me gut, me head started t' spin. Naggin' doubts entered me head, he was just too strong for me, Aa was almost ready t' give up, when...

GEORGE (V.O.)   Think Marky me lad, think strong, remember what yer told us?

A vision of Geordie appears, much to Marky's amazement.

MARKY:	What's that?
GEORGE:	My, your memory's short lad! Remember when yer said yer wanted t' be me, well, Aa've done all Aa can t' help yer. It's time t' go one better, it's time for yer t' be yersel', yer on yer own now Son! Remember this Marky, The Lion is dead, long live the Lion!
MARKY:	What...who, me?
GEORGE:	Aye, you Marky lad, The Byker Lion has been born! (vision and voice starts fading away), Farewell, an' try an' remember me, bonny lad an' tell them all who you really are!
MARKY:	Who me? Aa'm the Byker Lion, me!

V.O.

(music – Sabre Dance) A hidden power came through me, the likes of which Aa'd never felt before. (we see action) Grittin' me teeth, Aa gave out one almighty heave. Up and over he went, like a sack of tatties, landin' on his back with the wind knocked out of him. Aa did a little celebratory war-dance, the rest of the class gave a massive cheer, then Mr. Hearty jumped t' his feet, full of Hell, an' when he saw me grinnin' from ear t' ear, well, Aa think that made it all the worse. He couldn't wait for revenge! When we came t' grips again, almost at once yer could hear a pin drop. He went at me like a mad-man, tryin' his utmost t' drop me, an' judgin' by his mighty grip an' his snarlin', he was tryin' t' do some damage in the process. Neither of us gave an inch, on and on we went as though our very lives depended on the outcome. It had now became more than just a playful tussle on the mat, if it ever was that, no, now it was a battle of wills, undeclared war, the educated middle-class against the thick-headed, scrawny, less than workin' class! He had t' win, it had become a matter of honour and pride, and me, well, honour was for them that could afford it, an' Aa was too raggy-arsed for pride. Aa knew Aa had him rattled, an' for just one split second, he relaxed his grip. That's when Aa saw me chance, an' with all me strength an' power, which Aa never knew Aa had, Aa heaved him like Aa'd heaved many a bag of coal, onto me shoulder, at the same time Aa went down on one knee an' drove him with all me might, head first, with a sickenin' thud into the mat. He never moved. He lay there sparked out, white-faced, the same look about him that me Granda' had the day he passed away. Aa can remember thinkin', 'My God, Aa've went an' killed poor old Mr. Hearty, Aa wonder if they'll hang us?' Fortunately, thank the Lord, he opened his eyes. Well man, yer should have seen the look on his face, as he lay there, spread-eagled on the floor, with me standin' over him with me mucky feet an' baggy shorts. It must have hurt his pride more than anything, especially with all the others bayin' for his blood, shoutin' me t' finish him off. It's funny how everybody loves t' see the mighty fall, especially if it just so happens t' be the P.T. Teacher who thrives on humiliatin' his pupils. Without thinkin', Aa offered him an outstretched hand t' help him to his feet, he took it, but Aa still expected a tongue-lashin'. He was a far better man than Aa had given him credit for. He just gave me a good honest smile, an' Aa could tell by the look in eyes, he meant it. Then he patted me on the back an' shook me hand, almost dislocatin' me shoulder in the process, an' when he said with feelin'…

MR. HEARTY:　　　　Well done Son!

Well, Aa'll tell yer this for nowt, t' me it meant more than a knighthood an' a Victoria Cross rolled into one. In less than five minutes, Aa'd grown from a boy to a man. There was no gannin' back! Aa'd won the respect of many, Aa had become a local hero, all the kids wanted t' know me as Aa walked home from school that day still swollen with pride (we see Marky strutting down the street, surrounded by hangers' on)

We see Marky, chest puffed out, arrogant look on his face, enter the back door.
Well, how the mighty fall! Aa was soon brought back down t' earth. Me

Motha', the sneaky old bugger, was hidin' behind the back door, waitin' t' pounce. Aa came in, still full of mesel', an' walked straight into her powerful arms. She grabbed me by the scruff of the neck, an' with one mighty heave, lifted me off the floor, shakin' me like a rag doll. When Aa was blue in the face, she dropped me like a stone. Aa landed on me back, lyin' on the coconut mat on the scullery floor, with me Motha', hands on hips, lookin' down at the now fallen hero.

MA' (full of Hell): An' don't you hit wor Brian any more, or Aa'll bloody well kill yer!

V.O.

Well, there was no arguin' with her when she was in that kind of mood. She might have put the boot in when Aa was down, or in her case, the slipper. My, she's a bloody dirty fighter, me Ma', Aa'm sure she could have learnt old Geordie Hackenschmidt a thing or two!

(We see Marky in the bedroom) As lay on me bed goin' through the events of the day in my mind, it didn't seem real, more like a dream. Geordies picture looked down on me, smilin', Aa could have sworn that just this mornin' it was snarlin'. Aa felt marvellous, bloody well great, Aa felt like a World Champion, the 'Byker Lion!', aye that was me alright. Afraid of no one, Hah, well except me Motha', God bless her, but then again, yer can't count her can yer? She doesn't bloody fight fair!

From that day on Aa had a whole different outlook on life. Aa saved up an bought a new pair of gym shoes an' washed me feet before every P.T. lesson. Mr. Hearty wasn't such a bad fella' when yer really got t' know him. He was the only bloke who ever learnt me anything about life, well, apart from Geordie Hackenschmidt, an' his little red book!

We see Hackenschmidts' picture on the wall, smiling, and gives a wink.

(Cut to the street) We see Marky ambling proudly down the road, disappearing into the distance. (to the music Nimrod).

The End

The Byker Lion
Produced by Ron Moll
On 11th Aug 2009 – My 70th year.

The Byker Flash

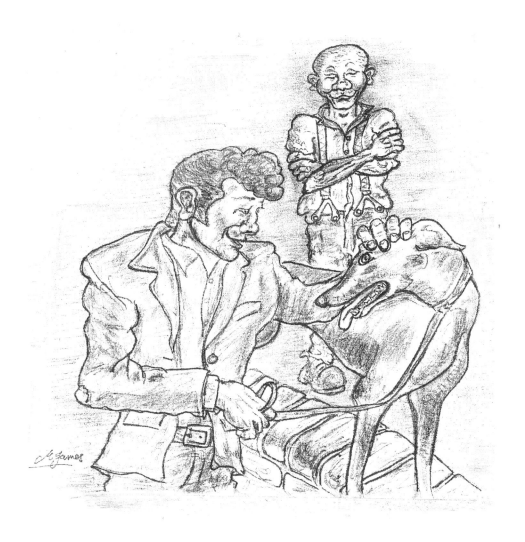

By Mark James

'THE BYKER FLASH'

by

Mark James

Characters:--

SID;   16 years old. Greased back hair with sideburns. Tony Curtis type. Teddy boy. Jack the lad.

DAVY; 14 years old. Shaven head. Tatty clothes. Short pants & braces. Hob nail boots. Bit of a tough guy.

TOMMY;   11 years old. Short back & sides. Tatty clothes. Short, baggy pants & snake belt. Black, holey sandshoes. Innocent. Talks with nervous stammer

DA';   Thin, bald. String vest. Flat cap. Woodbine on bottom lip. Mug of tea in hand. Lives for drinking & gambling.

MA';   Plump, curly-haired. Flowered pinny. Always busy.

UNCLE JOE;   Rag man. Wide boy. Horse & cart.

MAN in Quarry;   Unkempt, long, dirty Trench coat. Walks with stoop.

QUASSIE;   The Dog. Big, black, shaggy Greyhound. Looks more like a Wolfhound

Place:--

Byker, Newcastle, in the 50's. Hilly, cobbled streets & lanes. Tumbledown houses, gas-lamps, belching chimneys.

***

(We see, from a distance, the outside of a shabby picture hall)

DAVY V.O.

"There were six cinemas in old Bykers' square mile alone. As young uns', we lived an' breathed the flicks. We'd never miss a Sat'day screenin' of the latest movie, whether a Western, Gangster film, comedy or just a soppy old love story, we'd be there."

(We beam in to a close up of a poster advertising 'The Wizard of Oz')

"Whatever the film, the characters took possession of our very souls. We became part of the fantasy, a million miles away from the belchin' chimneys and cobbled lanes outside."

(We see the three brothers in the picture hall, their faces lit up by the flickering film. On screen we see Dorothy, the Tin man, the Lion and the Scarecrow dancing down the yellow brick road, followed closely by Toto, to the song of 'Follow the yellow brick road' We see a close up of Sid, wide-eyed and lovestruck)

"There was Sid, me older brother, he was a bit of a Jack-the lad, always tryin' t' make a quick few bob for doin' as little as possible. (We see a close up of Dorothy) Sixteen he was an' he always had a glint in his eye when the leadin' lady was on!" (We see Sid again)

SID: (Lovestruck, shaking head from side to side) Boy, Aa wish Aa had a dame!

(We see a close up of Tommy, hypnotised to the screen)

"And then there was wor young un', Tommy, 11 he was an' he always wanted t' take the animals home. (We see a close up of Toto) If he had his way, Aa'm sure Champion the wonder Horse would be sharin' me garden shed with King Kong." (We see Tommy again)

TOMMY: Aa w..w..wish we had a D..D..D..Dog!

(We see a close up of Davy, smiling)

"An' finally there was me, 14 Aa was at the time, an' addicted t' the big screen, (We see a close up of the Scarecrow) **my only escape from school."**

DAVY: (Joking) Aa wish Aa had a brain!

***

(We see from a distance a semi-detached Council house, with Ma' scrubbing the front step and Da' digging a leek trench)

"We'd only just recently moved house. It'd seemed a million miles away, on the back of Uncle Joes' Horse an' cart, leavin' the tumbledown, soot-blackened, back to back houses with the netty in the yard, enterin' a new world of hot runnin' water, three bedrooms and even a garden!...

(We see a living room scene. Da' sits, ear glued to the wireless, marking his football pools. He curses every result)

...We all loved it, we had the best of both worlds. Our old haunts an' playmates were just five minutes up the road. But Da', he hated it. "Too bloody far from the boozer an' the bookies." He'd moan. Da' was a hard drinkin' an' gamblin' man, but like most gamblers, he was a born loser!"

DA':   (Cursing) We've had no friggin' luck since we moved int' this bloody hoose!

(In the kitchen, Ma' is preparing food)

MA':   (Sarcastic) Ee, he's a treasure he is, Aa only wish some bugger would go an' bury him, bloody evil swine from hell!

(From the back lane, a bugle calls)

DA': (Jumps) For God's sake, there's never no bloody peace in this hoose! One of these days Aa'm gonna shove that old bugle so far up wor Joe's arse that when he farts yer'd think Dizzy Gillespie's in toon!

MA': Your Joe always did blow his own trumpet.

(The full-time results finish, Da' crumples up pools coupon and throws them into the fire)

DA': Bastard!!! It's this hoose Aa'm tellin' yer, it's friggin' cursed, roll on bloody openin' time!

(We see Uncle Joe, trundling up the lane, with his Horse and cart, blowing his bugle)

***

(Later that evening, we see Sid, Davy and Tommy coming out of the cinema. They thread their way along the main road. As they go they mimic the action from the film. Tommy struggles to keep up with them)

ALL: (Singing) WE'RE OFF T' SEE THE WIZARD, THE WONDERFUL WIZARD OF OZ...

SID: (Funny walk) Willyer look at me, Aa'm the Tin man!

DAVY: (Jokingly) Aye, an' if yer don't watch yersel', we'll weigh yer in for scrap iron!

SID: Oh Aye, me Uncle Joe would love that, he'd give yer nowt but a balloon for a Ton of gold that stingy owld git!

DAVY: (Laughs) We wouldn't even get that off him, tight as a bloody Camels arse in a sandstorm he is! If he was a ghost he wouldn't even give yer a fright unless yer paid for it!

SID: Ooo, don't mention ghosts in front of wor Tommy man, he's scared of his own shadow he is!

DAVY: (To Tommy) BOO!!!

TOMMY: (Jumps) Aaghh!!! D..d..divvent do that m..man, Aa'll tell me M..M..Ma' on ye!

DAVY: (Goes into scarecrow-like walk) Ah, cheer up man, yer miserable little shit. Look at me Aa'm the Scarecrow.

SID: (Joking) Aye, yer right there turnip-heed, yer face would frighten the vultures off a dead donkey!

TOMMY: C..c..can Aa be the L..L..L..Lion then, eh, c..can Aa?

SID: Can yer imagine that, wor Tommy a Lion, king of the jungle an' all that. Aa tell yer tho', yer definitely need some courage, yer ever seen a Lion scared of his own shadow?

DAVY: Aye, an' yer'd have t' grow yer hair an' all, Tommy. Aa've never seen a Lion with such a dodgy hair cut!

SID: Tell yer what, Tommy, yer always wanted a Dog, why not be Toto, yer could take yersel' for a walk in the park an' piss up the nearest tree.

TOMMY: N..n..no, Aa'm not bein' a D..D..Dog, Aa wanna be a Lion!

(The lads arrive at the Chippy)

TOMMY:	(Inhaling aroma of Chippy) Aa'm s..s..starvin', we gettin' some chips or what, S..S..Sid?
SID:	Naw, we're needin' t' be gettin' on home, anyhows', we're spent up, we've got nothin' left!
TOMMY:	(Pleading) Aw, c'mon, m..m..man, Aa'm starvin'.
SID:	'(Shaking Tommy gently by the ear) D'yer not listen, man, do Aa have t' spell it out? We've got no more friggin' money, man, chips cost money, yer haven't got any money, then yer can't have yer bloody chips, understand?
DAVY:	Anyway, king of the jungle, Aa thought Lions could go for weeks without food, an' as a matter of fact, when's the last time yer seen a bloody Lion eatin' a bag of chips, eh?
SID:	(Laughing) Aye, don't worry, Lion, it's Sat'day night, so Ma'll have a pan of broth on, they reckon Lions would kill for me Ma's broth.
TOMMY:	Ma's b..b..broth, Aa d..d..d..didn't know Lions ate broth!
SID:	Yer've got a lot t' learn Lion.
DAVY:	(Starting a run) Aa can almost smell me Ma's broth from here, last one gets none!

(Sid starts off into a run, following Davy, leaving Tommy behind)

TOMMY:	W..w..wait for me, Aa'll tell me Ma!

(The lads slow down, laughing)

DAVY: Howay, man, hurry up 'Tommy the bloody Lionheart', or we'll end up lickin' the empty bowl!

(Tommy catches up to them. It's dark, the pavement is wet, the street is lit by gas lamps. The brothers walk away from us, arms around each others' shoulders. Singing with feeling)

ALL: SOMEWHERE, OVER THE RAINBOW, WAY UP HIGH...(As they disappear into the distance)

* * *

(Next day, early afternoon, entrance to Byker Quarry. Dirty, unshaven scoundrel-type comes down the road with big black Dog on a rope. Looks cautiously around before turning off into the Quarry, pulling the reluctant Dog)

MAN: (Cursing) Bad luck, yer nowt but friggin' bad luck, but luck's about t' change for me yer mangy mutt!

(He Drags the Dog towards the Quarry pond. The Dog yelps. He holds the Dog between his knees and ties a rock to the end of the rope)

MAN: Last time yer make a friggin' fool out of me!

(Sid passes the Quarry, fag dangling from the side of his mouth, and hears a splash. The man comes dashing out of the Quarry entrance, barging past Sid. Sid is about to travel on, but hesitates as he hears a whimpering from the Quarry. He turns into the Quarry to investigate. He is startled as he notices a Dog struggling in the pond, he spits out his fag)

SID: (Loud) Bloody hell!!!

(He flings off his coat as he breaks into a run. Takes his shoes off with a hop and a skip, falling over in the process. The Dog howls)

SID: (Yelling) Aa'm on me way Dog, hang on in there, Aa'm comin'!

(There is a loud splash as Sid dives in)

***

(Later, still in the Quarry, on dry land. Sid is sitting there petting the Dog. Davy ambles onto the scene, sees Sid with the Dog and gives them both a funny look)

DAVY: (Mockingly) How Sid, great movie yest'day weren't it. Aa see yer've found Toto, any sign of Dorothy? Starts laughing)

SID: Take the piss all yer like, kidda, Aa've found mesel' a rare old thoro'bred here. Feed him up a bit, train him, an' Aa'm on a certain winner wi' this one. He'll be the pride of Brough Park within a month. Who knows, Davy lad, he might even make the big time an' get t' White City! (Stops and thinks for a second) Aa'll even have him catchin' Rabbits in the dene, that'll keep me Motha' an' Fatha' happy, A Dog that brings yer bloody Sunday dinner in!

DAVY: (Busy chucking stones into the Quarry pond, in a world of his own, bombing the Germans, every bomb is a hit) Weeeee-kabooooom!!! And Dresden bites the dust as Bomber Harris' squadron wipes out yet another...

SID: (Interrupting Davy, curled up lip) Hey, knuckle-nose, d' yer hear what Aa'm sayin'?

DAVY: (Turns away from the pond and faces Sid) Why aye, man, he's a bloody champion he is, Sid, a world-beater if Aa ever saw one. Aa've never seen such a healthy lookin' beast in me life!

(We see a close up of the Dog, skinny and matted. Davy gives it a good going over)

"Why man, yer should've seen it, me, Aa couldn't believe me eyes, it was sort of unnatural lookin' like, yer know, a bit of a misfit it was. For a start, it's body was far too short for those long, skinny, misshapen legs. It had a long, thin snout with these beady, starin' eyes that were too far apart. Aa wasn't sure what colour it was, 'cos its' wet, smelly coat had dried all matted and spiky, like an overgrown sewer Rat!"

DAVY:	Hey Sid, Aa know yer fond of Dogs an' all that, like, but this one's in a bit of a state an' yer can smell it before yer see it, man, it smells like it's been dead for three months! (Laughs to himself) Take the poor bugger t' the Cat an' Dog shelter an' put it out its' bloody misery, at least it'd get fed there!
SID:	Ah, shut yer bloody mooth an' give yer arse a chance yer heartless little gob-shite, what the poor bugger needs is a home an' a carin' owner, someone t' love him an' nurture him. Aa'm tellin' yer, he's got real breedin' potential this one has, Aa could make a few bob studdin' him!
DAVY:	(Laughing) Breedin' my arse! (Nods and points to the dog) An' what's it s'posed t' be like, what make?
SID:	(Laughs and playfully punches Davy on the shoulder) Yer mean breed, yer daft bugger! What breed is it?
DAVY:	Well breed then, what sort of breed's it s'posed t' be?
SID:	What d'yer think, eh? What's it look like bonehead!

DAVY:	(Shrugs) Beats me!

(The lads pet and inspect the Dog closely)

"If wor Sid hadn't of told us, Aa would never have took it for a Racin' Dog. (Laughs) A bloody Greyhound, Aa couldn't believe it. T' tell the truth, Aa don't know what Aa would've taken it for. Aa know one thing tho', Aa would have left the ugly mutt t' fend for itsel'. But wor Sid, he's got a bit of a soft spot for animals, 'specially if he thinks there's a bit of a profit t' be made!"

DAVY:	Anyway, where'd yer find him? Don't tell us Crufts!
SID:	(Non the wiser) Naw, Aa went an' picked him out of the Quarry pond, (Nodding his head to Dog) didn't Aa, Son!
DAVY:	Why?
SID:	'Cos he was bloody drownin' wasn't he, yer barmy wooden-heeded bugger!
DAVY:	Drownin'! Aa find that hard t' believe!
SID:	An' how's that like?
DAVY:	(Demonstrating Doggie paddle) 'Cos all Dogs can swim, can't they!
SID:	Not with a bloody rope tied 'round his neck he couldn't!
DAVY:	(Laughs and shakes head) A rope, that wouldn't stop him swimmin'!
SID:	It didn't, but Aa think the bloody great rock tied t' the other end might of!

DAVY:	(Laughs aloud) It's no wonder the mutt looks sick of his life, poor bugger. He's just went an' tried t' do himsel' in, sick of his bloody life, he tries t' end it all, then Tarzan, Lord of the Quarry comes along an' pulls him out of the drink an' saves the bloody day!
SID:	Are yer tryin' t' be funny yer little shit!
DAVY:	(Laughing) Calm down man, Aa'm only jokin', but talk about funny, Sid, (Nods towards Dog) he's the funniest lookin' Dog Aa've ever seen in me life!
SID:	(Looking hurt) An' how d' yer make that out, like?
DAVY:	For a start, is he s'posed t' have that hump?
SID:	What hump?
DAVY:	(Pointing) There, look, right there, that thing on its' back, that bloody hump!
SID:	(Kneels, strokes the Dogs back tenderly) That's never a hump, (Thinks hard) that's all Goddamn muscle that is!
DAVY:	Giver over, man, (Sarcastically) Aa've seen 'The Hunchback of Notre Dam' three bloody times, an' Aa'm tellin' yer, that's definitely a hump if Aa ever saw one!
SID:	(Smiling with satisfaction, moves proudly towards the Dog) Will yer just take a look at them legs, man, bloody runnin' legs they are!

(Davy laughs, shaking his head)

SID:	An' what are yer laughin' at now, what's so funny, eh?
DAVY:	(Bending closer) Oh, nowt, it's just, er, are they s'posed t' be that shape, like?
SID:	What shape?
DAVY:	Well, bow-legged at the back an' knock-kneed at the front!
SID:	(Puzzled, rubbing chin thoughtfully) Yeah.
DAVY:	Yeah what?
SID:	(Thinking hard) Yeah, course they're s'posed t' be that shape!
DAVY:	(Mockingly) Give over, man, Aa find that hard t' believe.
SID:	(Pondering) Yeah, well, er, well it stands t' reason doesn't it? It's obvious!
DAVY:	(Laughing) Stands t' reason, my arse! They should call ye 'Sewer Sid', 'cos yer so full of bloody shit! C'mon then, what's so bloody obvious?
SID:	Well, think about it man, if his front legs weren't knock-kneed, an' his back legs weren't bandy, then, er…
DAVY:	Howay then Einstein, give us yer bloody theory!
SID:	…er, it's common sense, like…

(Sid squats on his haunches, knees wide apart, leans forward and demonstrates, moving his arms between open legs)

SID: ...think about it, man, if his legs weren't that shape, how for Christs' sake could he run...

(Sid straightens up rubbing the small of his back with one hand and pointing to the Dogs' testicles with the other, nodding his head triumphantly)

SID: ...without hittin' himsel' in the bollocks!

(Davy laughs loudly)

SID: Aa'm friggin' tellin' yer, man, no shit, swear on wor Tommy's life!

DAVY: (Scarcastically) Calm down man, Sid, Aa believe yer, honest, tho' many wouldn't! (Starts laughing and recites) "And the Elephant is a dainty bird, it hops from bough to bough, it builds its' nest in a Rhubarb tree and it whistles like a Cow!"

(They both start laughing, then the Dog farts, and they laugh harder)

DAVY: (In between infectious laughter) He's just like ye, wor Sid, full of wind an' shit!

(They both roll around in laughter, holding their sides, tears streaming down their faces)

***

(Early evening, in the back garden, we see Sid, Davy and Tommy with the Dog, the back door is open)

SID: Hope me Fatha's not in!

DAVY: Aa bet he is, it's not openin' time at Raby for another hour!

SID:	Tell yer what, if me Motha's in, Aa'll ask, an' if me Fatha's in, (Winks at Davy) ye ask, an' if they're both in wor Tommy...
TOMMY:	Aye?
SID:	(Pushing Tommy forward) ...ye can ask!
TOMMY:	Why m..m..me?
SID:	'Cos me Da' knows how much yer love Dogs, anyhow, yer the bloody youngest, now get in before Aa put me foot up yer arse!
TOMMY:	But it's a..a..always me!
DAVY:	Just put yer sad look on, man Tommy, me Fatha'll fall for it straight away, he always does wi' ye!

(We see Da' standing at the open door, braces dangling, string vest on and pot of tea in hand)

DA':	(Looks at Dog, sarcastic) An' what the friggin' hell d' yer call that then?
TOMMY:	It's a D..D..D..Dog, Da', a real D..D..Dog!
DA':	For Christs' sake, Aa can see it's a friggin' Dog, yer bloody idiot!

(Ma' arrives behind Da')

MA':	Ahh, will yer look at the state of it, poor little thing, looks half-starved it does, an' it could do wi' a bath, poor little bugger.
DA':	An' where the bloody Hell did yer find the mangy thing?

TOMMY:	It f..f..followed us home Da', d..d..d..didn't it wor Sid. Can we k..k..keep it, Ma', c..c..can we keep it, eh, please?
MA':	Well Aa'm not too sure, yer'll have t' ask yer Da'.
DA':	Like shite, there's no bloody Dog comin' in this friggin' hoose, don't yer think we've got enough bloody mouths t' feed, eh!
TOMMY:	(Begging) B..b..but Da'!
DA':	But nowt! Aa've said it once, an' Aa'll say it again, there's no bloody Dog comin' in this friggin' hoose! That's the end of it!

(Da' turns on his slippered heel, spilling his tea and cursing as he goes back in the house)

MA':	(To Sid) An' where the bloody Hell have ye been wor Sidney, yer soaked through t' the skin?
SID:	(Joking) Me Ma'? Er, Aa've just been for a swim.
MA':	An' where would that be, like?
SID:	Shipley Street baths, Ma'.
MA':	With all yer bleedin' clothes on?
SID:	Aye, Ma', Aa forgot me bather.
MA':	(Laughs) Yer stupid bugger, yer should be settin' an example t' yer younger brothers, go an' get changed afore yer catch yer death!

***

(In the back garden, in an old, wooden shed, Sid, Woodbine dangling,

69

gangster style, from the side of his mouth, grooms the Dog. Davy looks on, pulling faces)

"Well, me Fatha' did say there was no Dog gettin' in his hoose, but he said nowt about the garden shed, which was our 'Gang hut'. Aa couldn't believe me ears when wor Sid named the Dog. Aa thought he said Rat at first, but no, can yer believe it, Aa had t' laugh, he only went an' called it bloody 'Flash'! A Dog was a Dog t' young Tommy, he called it 'Lassie', he obviously hadn't noticed its' bollocks! The Dog was ugly, an' definitely had a hump, me, Aa had t' call him 'Quassimodo'!"

(The Dog looks up at Davy, almost grinning, wagging it's tail)

DAVY: (Laughs) Look at him, he's got a bloody good right t' laugh an' all, with ye feedin' him on the best mince all the time. We're bloody lucky if we get drippin' an' bread!

SID: (Stroking Dog) Aye, but it'll be worth it when he's a champion tho', Davy, ye wait an' see. Yer a good lad, Flash, aren't yer, yer a good lad alright!

(Sid stands up and looks at his reflection in the hut window, and combs his hair)

SID: Aye, he's gonna be a champion alright, Aa'm tellin' yer, a good investment, Aa say, ye mark my words! He just needs the right trainin' an' plenty of food t' build him up, (pause) aye, it'll cost a few bob t' feed him up tho', but he'll pay for himself' after a couple of races!

(Sid walks over to Davy, and puts his arm around Davys' neck, in a show of affection, and gives him a brotherly hug)

DAVY: (Twisting face) Get off us yer big daft shite! Yer after somethin' Aa bet, c'mon, what d' yer want?

SID:	(Innocent, points to himself) Who, me?
DAVY:	Aye, ye, what yer after?
SID:	(Smiles) Well, there's non flies on ye, wor kid, (Jokes) but yer can see where they've been. (Change of mood, more serious, back to combing hair, busy with the parting) Hey Davy, Aa've been thinkin' like, Aa know we have our disagreements, the occasional fall out an' all that, but how about ye an' me bein' partners, eh, fifty, fifty split.
DAVY:	(Sarcastic) Oh aye, me part with me money while ye part yer hair!

(Scene flashes back)

"Head in the cloud has wor kid, but yer had t' give him his dues. He always had a thing about Dogs, well, Racin' Dogs that is. He used t' work at Brough Park, the local Greyhound stadium just down the road. Was his first job, 15 he was, just left school, Kennel boy, he loved it. Wouldn't think when yer look at him now, but Wor Sid used t' be shy. Like most kids, he was at home in the company of animals rather than people. They reckon he could just about talk t' the Dogs, as if he understood what they were sayin', like. He knew their mood swings, when they felt low an' when they were up, an' ready t' race. The wide-boys soon got t' know about Sids' understandin' with the Dogs. Every gamblin' man in Byker begged him for tips, an' with him bein' shy an' innocent, he was easy meat for the blood suckin' leeches.

He wasn't doin' anythin' wrong, it made him feel important, he was easily led on tho'. Mind yer, he never placed any bets on himsel', for a start he wouldn't have a clue how t' put a bet on, he could hardly read an' write, let alone reckon up!

The Bookies on the track took a right hidin'. They got wind of wor Sid, an' put the boot in. It was easily done, they accused him of, huh, can yer believe this, they accused him of bloody dopin' the favourite, which came in last. All the money was on the outsider, which romped home at six-to-one. Broke his heart when they sacked him on the spot.

As yer can see, he's older and wiser now, but still as daft on Racin' Dogs, the first love of his life! Daft bugger, never learnt, never will!"

(Sid is on his haunches, stroking the dog, dreamily. Davy joins him, puts a hand on Sids shoulder sympathetically)

DAVY: (With feeling) He's not much t' look at, Sid, is he, Aa mean, if yer owned a Race Horse, yer wouldn't wan't it t' look like a pack Mule, would yer?

SID: (Hurt) What yer on about, eh? Anyway, looks can be deceivin'.

DAVY: True, but even so, he doesn't even look like a Racin' Dog t' me. Don't let yer heart rule yer head, man.

SID: (Raising voice) An' what's that s'posed t' mean, like?

"Wor Kid tries on a Camel-Hair overcoat Four sizes too big!"

DAVY:	Well man, just forget about Greyhound racin', eh. Aa mean he'll make a good pet an' all that, but a Racin' Dog, t' tell the truth Sid, Aa've never heard anythin' so ridiculous in me bloody life!
SID:	(Mad) Anyway, What d' ye know about Racin' Dogs, eh? Aa'll bloody tell yer, yer know nowt!
DAVY:	(Gestures with open hands) Hold on a minute Sid, man, Aa'm only tryin' t' give yer me opinion, as yer partner, like.
SID:	Opinion, Aa don't want yer bloody opinion, if Aa wanted yer bloody opinion Aa'd bloody well ask for yer opinion right, clever shite!
DAVY:	Calm down, man. Just hold yer horses, (Laughs), er, Aa mean Dog.
SID:	Aye, funny bugger aren't yer!
DAVY:	Seriously tho' Sid, just answer us one question Aa've been dyin' t' ask. No offence, like, but how the bloody Hell d' yer know the Dog can run, never mind bloody race?
SID:	(Shaking his head) Run?

(We see an imaginary scene of a Greyhound race in slow motion, as the Dogs, stride for stride, pursue the Hare)

"**Wor kid looked really hurt. He couldn't believe for a second that anyone, 'specially me, his kid brother, was daft enough t' doubt his judgement. Like Aa says, he'd worked at the Dogs an' told me a thousand times, in his own words, "Aa know more about Greyhoond Racin' than all the fat-bellied owners an' piss-head trainers put t'gether"."**

SID:	(As if waking from a dream. In a John Wayne drawl) Run, it certainly can, like the Goddam wind, pardner, ye watch the Son of a gun go, he'll run like the bloody wind, an' yer better believe it!

(Sid gets up and swaggers over to Davy. He flicks his cigarette over the fence. Turns his coat collar up. Pursed lip curled under his teeth.

SID:	(Bogardesque) An' yer better believe it kid!

(He puts two fingers to his mouth and whistles to the Dog)

"Aa don't think Quassie had been t' the pictures and seen Casablanca, 'cos he didn't come runnin', but then again, wor kid was no Lauren Bacall!"

***

(In the kitchen, Da' is reading the paper. Ma' is busy pottering and Tommy reads a comic)

DA':	(Peers over paper) What's gettin' int' them two daft buggers these days?
MA':	An' how d'yer mean, like?
DA':	Yer know what Aa mean, they're up t' bloody summat!
MA':	Like what? Give us a clue, Aa haven't got a crystal ball, yer know!
DA':	Well, they're actin' all funny like. Aa blames that bloody Dog, Aa do, what d' they call it?
TOMMY:	(Looks up) Lassie, Da', his name's L...L...Lassie.
DA':	What? Are ye takin' the bloody piss or what!

TOMMY:	Naw, why l...l...like?
DA':	Lord forgive us for me bloody sins, it's a friggin' Dog, willick brain!
TOMMY:	So, Lassie was a D...D...D...Dog.
DA':	(Looks skyward) Lord spare us, Aa bloodywell give up Aa does!
MA':	The bairn can't help it, man, yer bloody bad tempered sod. All Dogs are Dogs t' him, sex doesn't come int' it.
TOMMY:	Sex, what's sex?

(Ma' gives Tommy a clip around the ear)

TOMMY:	Ooouch!
MA':	Don't talk dirty in this house, (She turns to Da') anyway, wor Sid named the Dog Flash, but Davy calls him Quassie, an' like yer heard, Tommy here calls him Lassie, so bloody sort that one out.
DA':	Jee-sus Christ woman, it's no bloody wonder the Dog's daft, it doesn't even know it's own bloody name. All the same, Aa'll tell yer summat for nowt, there's been no bloody luck since that mangy mongrel came int' this house!
TOMMY:	It's not a m...m...mongrel, wor S...S...Sid reckons it's a what d' yer call it Ma?
MA':	A pedigree, Son.
DA':	Pedigree my friggin' arse!

TOMMY:	Anyhow, you w...w...won't even let it in the h...h... house, it lives in the g...g...garden shed, an' wor Sid, Davy and me l...l...look after it, don't we Ma!
DA':	Oh aye, well yer want t' try feedin' the hungry bugger an' gettin' it friggin' toilet trained, it only eats me onions an' pisses on me prize leeks. An' another thing, Aa don't like the way it bloodywell looks at us!
MA':	What d' yer mean?
DA':	Yer know, the bloody evil eye, woman!
MA':	Silly bugger, the poor thing's cross-eyed!
DA':	That's another bloody thing, isn't it, a friggin' cock-eyed Dog! People will laugh, man, Aa'm tellin' yer, we'll be the talk of the bloody wash-hoose we will!
TOMMY:	B...b...but Da', Sid says it's a p...proper Racin' Dog, isn't it, M...M...Ma', tell him, go on, Ma', t...t...tell him.
MA':	Aye, Son, it's one of them Greyhound things.
TOMMY:	Aye, an' wor S...Sid r...r...reckons it's gonna be a champion, s...so there.
DA':	(Sarcastic) A champion, ha, don't make me bloody laugh. If that ugly, humpy-backed Mutt is a Greyhound, then Aa'm bloody Dick Barton, Special bloody Agent. (Looks at clock) Shit, it's nearly bloody openin' time, ye an' that stupid friggin' Dog!

***

"Wor kid organised the trainin' on Byker Park...

(Byker Park. Sid stands there, all official. Davy, bent forward, holds the Dog, by the collar, between his knees. Tommy, holey black sandshoes, wearing raggy-arsed shorts, stands at the ready some fifty yards away, holding a length of string, with a Rabbit skin on the end)

...What a laugh, it kills me just t' think about it. Wor young un', as usual, was the Guinnea Pig, or should Aa say Hare."

SID:	(Cups hands to mouth and shouts) Yer ready wor Tommy?
TOMMY:	Aye, Aa'm is.
SID:	(Louder) Steady...

(Tommy gets ready to run)

SID:	(Top of his voice ...GO!!!

(Tommy runs like hell, dragging the Rabbit skin behind him on a length of string. At the same time, Davy lets go of the Dog)

SID:	(In admiration) Will yer look at him go, didn't Aa tell yer!

(Quassie soon makes up the ground on Tommy, catches the Rabbit skin, shakes it, drops it and continues to run after Tommy, who is still running with the piece of string, minus the skin. Quassie closes Tommy down and sinks his teeth into Tommys' raggy arse)

TOMMY:	(Screams) Aaaargh!!!

(Quassie returns to Sid, proudly, with the remains of Tommys' raggy trousers in his mouth)

SID:	(Patting the Dog) Good lad, what are yer, Flash, yer a good lad!

(Quassie barks and wags his tail excitedly)

"Now wor young un's no Jessie Owens, but he's no slouch either...

(We see Tommy run the same race in slow motion, grim determination etched on his face, as he looks over his shoulder to the advancing Dog, to the music of Chariots of Fire)

...He'd won the hundred yards dash, the egg an' spoon race, the sack race an' he came second in the three-legged race in the schools sports day. But Quassie, well, he certainly surprised me with his speed, made wor Tommy look like he was standin' still."

DAVY: Pretty impressive, like, but Aa still think we're floggin' a dead horse here, Sid Aa know the Dog looked fast an' all that, but it don't really prove nowt, after all, wor Tommy's no Greyhound, is he?

TOMMY: Aye, an' me M...M...Ma'll bloody well k...kill us when she sees the s...s...state of me troosers!

SID: (Thinking hard) Shut up man, yer wingin' little shit, Aa'm tryin' t' bloody think man.

(Slow smile spreads across Sids face)

SID: (To Davy) Yer know what?

DAVY: What?

SID: For once in yer life yer bloodywell right, Aa reckon it's time for the real thing, definitely the real bloody thing!

***

(Brough Park, early morning, just getting light. We see three blackened-faced Commandos crawl through a hole in the fence. On the track, at the start-cum-finish line, Davy, back bent, holds the dog between his knees. Sid is at his side, looking important. He half turns and looks over his shoulders. In one hand he holds a stop watch at eye level, he puts two fingers to his mouth. We hear a loud shrill whistle. The mechanical Hare comes flying around the track and flashes past Sid and Davy)

SID: (Shouts in Davy's ear) They're off!

(Davy lets go of the Dog. The Dog races round the track after the Hare. We see the Dog in full stride)

"Quassie took off like a rocket, all his awkwardness was left behind. We looked on in admiration....

(Close up of the lads' faces, we see pure joy)

...Quassies' movements were fluent and smooth...

(We see the Dog in slow motion)

...he had rhythm, balance an' grace as he swept 'round the bend, becomin' a vision of pure beauty. On the straight, his speed took our breath away. In a blur he zoomed 'round the race-track. Aa didn't bother t' ask the lap time, t' tell the truth, Aa'd be non the wiser. All the same, Aa'd a feelin' that this Dog could run, but Aa needed an experts opinion."

DAVY: Well Sid, is he fast then, eh? What d' yer reckon?

SID: (Gives an appreciative whistle then shakes his head) Aa'm not even goin' t' bother answerin' a daft bloody question like that!

                                         ***

(We see the boys walking home with the Dog)

DAVY: Well, is he? Go on tell us!

79

SID:	(Smoking) Is he what?
DAVY:	Yer know what Aa mean!
SID:	(Sarcastic) Not really, Aa can't read yer bloody mind, can Aa?
TOMMY:	(Innocent) Is Lassie f...f...fast. Well, is he wor k...k...kid?
DAVY:	(Impatiently) Will yer answer the bairn, he's askin' yer a question, was Quassie fast or what?
SID:	(Grinning, leans on Davys' shoulder, and rubs his head) Oh aye tattie-heed, he can gan a bit, (He then grabs Davy and Tommy by the ears, laughs, and gives them an over-friendly shake) it can certainly bloody shift alright, an' Aa'm sick of tellin' ye two nuggets, his name's Flash, (Nodding his head dreamily) the Byker Flash!

***

(In the kitchen, Da' read the paper, Tommy comes in all excited)

TOMMY:	Yer should've s...s...seen it go, whoosh!
DA':	See what?
TOMMY:	(Proudly) Wor Racin' D...D...D...dog.
DA':	Oh aye, bloody Racin' Dog yer say?
TOMMY:	Aye, it's really fast, Da'.
DA':	Aye, sure, bloody Rin Tin Tin's fast, but doesn't make him a friggin' Racin' Dog, does it?

TOMMY:	But y...yer should've seen it, m...m...man, whooooosh!

(He demonstrates with his hands)

DA':	(Looking over his paper) Naa, don't talk bloody daft, man, it only seems fast because it's runnin' on it's own, there's nowt t' compare it with. Don't let yer imagination run away with yer, Son, yer get nowt for nowt these days, man, think about it, yer just don't find Racin' Dogs walkin' the streets, d' yer?
MA':	Ah man, leave the bairn alone, let him live his dreams, it does no bloody harm at his age.
DA':	Aye, but he's got t' learn the facts, doesn't he? Yer don't want the laddie growin' up daft like the other two, they're on another bloody planet most the time!
MA':	There's worse than them two, they do no one no harm d' they?
DA':	Aa blame bloody Sid, thinks he's a Jack the bloody lad he does, an' that stupid bloody Davy just follows in his footsteps, Like a bloody shadow he his. If Sid jumped off Byker Bridge, Aa bloody sure t' Hell reckon Davy would follow, friggin' barmy bugger!
TOMMY:	B...b...but Da' man, Aa'm not kiddin' yer, if y...y...yer'd only seen him at the p...p...park, like a Whippet he was!
DA':	(Interested) An' where was this park, like, Byker Park?

TOMMY:	Naw, don't be s...s...stupid, we was at B...B... Brough Park, man, an' wor S...S...Sid clocked him, an' he nearly caught the H...H...Hare!
DA':	Don't talk daft, an' don't ye call me bloody stupid, or Aa'll put me foot up yer arse!
TOMMY:	Honestly Da', cross me heart an' h...hope t' d...d... die.
DA':	Hmmm, so yer sayin' it ran all the way 'round the track, wor Sid timed it an' it gave the Hare a run for its' money?
TOMMY:	Aye, honest, Da'.
DA':	An' what was the time like?
TOMMY:	Err, about h...h...hap-past Six this mornin'!
DA':	Bloody daft shite! The friggin' lap time for Gods' sake.
TOMMY:	Oh, w...well Aa don't know, l...l...like, but wor Sid reckons it broke somethin'.
DA':	What! Broke somethin', that's all we bloody need now, friggin' Vets' bills, Aa told yer we'd had no luck since that bloody Dog arrived, wait 'til Aa get me bloody hands onit, Aa'll break somethin' alright, it's friggin' neck!
TOMMY:	A r...r...record, that's it, it b...b...broke some kind of record.
DA':	What! The track record?
TOMMY:	Aye, that's it, the t...t...track record.

DA':	Bloody hell, Aa told yer that Dog had potential, that's the thing about them Racin' Dogs, it's not what they look like, yer know, but what's inside them that counts, Aa knew he had it! Anyway Tommy, son, where's the Dog now?
TOMMY:	Err, with wor Sid an' D...D...Davy, Aa think.
DA':	Hmmm, it's gettin' on a bit, an' it's dark out there, Aa bloody hope they're takin' good care of the Flash.
MA':	'The' Flash?
DA':	(Proud) Aye, the Flash alright, the Byker bloody Flash.

***

(We see Horse & cart parked up at side of cobbled road. The cart is piled with an assortment of old clothes. Uncle Joe sits up on the cart, Sid rumages through the clothes eagerly)

"Wor kid revelled in the dream he'd had since he was 15, of gettin' his own back. 'Aa'll show them...' he always said, '...one of these days!'

That day had arrived, he reckoned, an' he was more than ready. Even so, he'd have t' look the part. Uncle Joe was the local Rag man, he'd had a good day. He'd been toutin' in the posh end of Heaton."

U. JOE:	(Giving encouragement) It's all good stuff this, Sidney lad, all good stuff, there's no bloody junk in this lot. This is yer lucky day this is, yer lucky bloody day.

(Sid tries on several large overcoats. He settles for a Camel-hair overcoat, four sizes too big)

U. JOE: (Enthusiastic) Look great, bloodywell looks great that Sidney, man. Made t' measure, Aa'd say, aye, made t' bloody measure.

(Sid knots the belt, and draws it tight around his waist. Looking pleased with himself)

U. JOE: (Taking the piss) Yer look the double of that what's-his-name, Sidney, yer know the fella' Aa mean, that Humphrey Bogarde fella', the bloody double of him, Aa say.

(Sid knots a white silk scarf around his neck, and then tries on a black, velvet trilby. He looks pleased with himself)

U. JOE: That's the icin' on the cake that is, Son, the icin' on the bloody cake. Aa tell yer what, Aa'm gonna have t' rob mesel' here, Sidney lad, we'll say ten bob for the lot, yer look a million dollars an' all Aa'm askin' for is ten bob, it's a bargain if Aa ever saw one that is, a bloody bargain!

(Sid's ready to shake on it, knowing he has a bargain)

DAVY: Give over Uncle Joe, yer thievin' git, this is family this is, not yer every day punter! Yer know wor kid's not workin', five bob for the lot.

U. JOE: Who's the bloody robber now? Aa've got a wife an' three kids' t' feed Aa have, a wife an' three bloody kids! Five bob, give over, man! Aa'm not a bloody charity Aa'm not. But Aa s'pose Aa'm is yer Uncle, tell yer what boys, seven an' six, an' that's yer last offer yer little bloody Jesse James's, yer!

DAVY: What! Seven an' six, yer'd dip a blind mans' beggin' bowl when he's not lookin' ye would! Anyway Uncle Joe, we've only got seven bob between us, haven't we Sid?

SID: (Impressed with Davy's haggling skills) Eh? Er, why aye Uncle Joe, man, that's all we've got left between us. We've been spendin' all our money on bloody Dog food, it's an expensive game this Greyhound racin' business!

U. JOE: (Holding hands up in defeat) Okay lads', okay, Aa give in, done, seven bob it is, (He spits on his open hand, Davy does the same and they shake on it) but it's bloody daylight robbery it is, bloody daylight robbery! Came from the posh end of Heaton did this gear, posh end of bloody Heaton!

(Sid strikes a match with his thumbnail and lights a cigarette. Smiling with satisfaction, he proudly pulls the trilby down over his eyes. Cigarette dangling gangster style from his lips)

SID: (Bogarde drawl) Here's lookin' at yer, Uncle Joe, yer a good man.

U. JOE: Less of the bloody bullshit, Sidney lad, Aa'm currently seven bob short in me pocket, seven bob short, an' Aa don't do tick!

SID: (To Davy, Bogardesque) Well pardner, yer got the money for our good fella' here?

DAVY: (Smiling) Aye, Aa sure have, boss, he's certainly a good man, is our Uncle Joe, there's a place in heaven for him. Er, yer got change of ten bob, Uncle Joe?

U. JOE: (Laughing) Well yer little friggin' bugger yer! It's not often yer Uncle Joe comes second best in the hagglin' stakes, but yer've sure done me good an' proper this time, yer little sod yer, good an' bloody proper!

(Uncle Joes' horse inclines its' head in Sids' direction, and with a soft, rasping fart, shits on the cobbled road. Sid, too busy to notice the horses recent deposit, turns slowly, holding his lapels, and swaggers away. With a wet, soggy squelch, Sid steps into the fresh, steaming manure pile. Uncle Joe and Davy both start laughing as Sid continues to walk on down the street as if nothing had happened, occasionally flicking his right foot to get rid of the excess manure)

U. JOE:	Well Davy lad, been good doin' business with yer, an' good luck with the Dog. Aa'll be off now, a man's got t' make an honest livin' somehow, an' with little bloody highwaymen like ye around, it's an uphill battle all the way, an uphill bloody battle! (To horse) Gerrup!!! (They pull away)
DAVY:	Aye, cheers Uncle Joe, yer a hard man t' bargain with!

(They both start laughing. In the distance, Sid swaggers away, trying to preserve his dignity, now wiping his right shoe on a grass verge as he goes. Davy starts off to catch him up)

***

(In the living room, we see Da' reading his paper, Tommy enters the room)

DA':	Yer seen anythin' of that bloody Sid an' Davy?
TOMMY:	Aye, Aa think they t...t...took the D...D...Dog for a walk.
DA':	Oh aye, an' where would that be, don't tell us Brough Park again. (Laughs)
TOMMY:	Oh, er, naw, just the p...park.
MA':	What park? Byker, Heaton or Walker, it's pitch black out there!

TOMMY:	Er, Aa'm n...n...not sure.
DA':	Yer little bloody liar yer, what park they at?
TOMMY:	(Whispers) Er, Gosforth Aa think they s...s... says.
DA':	Speak up!
TOMMY:	G...G...Gosforth!
MA':	*(Worried)* What they went there for? Gosforth's miles away!
TOMMY:	Not that f...f...far on a Tram.
DA':	Two bloody Trams, yer've got t' change at Toon.
MA':	An' why would they be goin' all the way over there for?
TOMMY:	Said they were g...g...givin' Lassie a r...run out.
DA':	Like shite, Aa bet they're up t' bloody somethin'!
MA':	What time will they be back?
TOMMY:	Don't know.
DA':	Bloody answer yer Ma'!
TOMMY:	Oh, l...l...late-ish Aa suppose.
DA':	Nothin' but bloody trouble them two, Aa'm tellin' yer, yer tell them t' hop, an' yer can be guaranteed they'll either bloody skip or jump!
MA':	Calm yersel' down, will yer, ye finish readin' yer paper an' Aa'll make yer a pot of tea.

(Da' turns immediately to the racing page, we see a close up 'GOSFORTH PARK GREYHOUND RACING'. Da' starts weighing up the form)

DA':   (*Startled, choking and coughing on a draw of his cigarette*) Christ All-bloody-mighty! They've friggin' only went an' done it haven't they, the bloody crafty swines!

MA':   Done what?

DA':   Aa can't believe it, for Christs' sake, Aa can't bloody believe it!

MA':   Believe what?

DA':   The bloody 'Byker Flash' is only racin' at Gosforth Park the night! Aa always knew that Dog was a good un', the minute Aa set eyes on him, Aa thought, that one's a bloody champion, that one is, didn't Aa, eh?

MA':   Yer bloody liar!

DA':   (*Proud*) Aa always knew them lads o' mine would make somethin' of themselves, didn't Aa always say? They're gonna end up rich bloody business tycoons they are, Aa bet they'll not see their old fella' short in his old age.

MA':   Aa wouldn't count yer chickens yer old bloody hypocrite!

(We see Da' in the bedroom, he pulls his best suit out the wardrobe, and a Gold pocket watch on a chain out of the dressing table)

DA':   (*Shouting through to Ma'*) Yer just don't know d' yer, woman, can't yer bloody understand, that Dog not only went an' broke the track record at Brough Park, it bloody well smashed it t' smithereeeens! *(He comes back through to living room)* Tell yer what Son, *(Pats Tommy on the head, and hands him suit and watch)* run down t' Pawnship an' put these in for us, Aa want at least £10 for them mind yer, an' then run down t' the bookies before it closes an' put me bet on. *(As he writes out a betting slip)*

MA':   Bloody Hell, yer can't just go pawnin' yer Granda's watch, it's real gold that is an' worth a small bleedin' fortune, it's all he had left when he died, he'll be turnin' in his grave he will, an' that's yer best suit, for cryin' out loud man, have yer gone mad or what?

DA':   Gods' sake woman will yer shut yer friggin' mouth, man, Aa'm tellin' yer, it's a dead cert this one, an' at twelve to one it's goin' t' pay out well an' bloody proper! *(Hands Tommy betting slip and £5)* Now hurry up Son, there's a fifteen pound win on the Flash, *(Laughs)* Aa always knew that one was a winner, *(Tommy leaves with suit, watch, money and betting slip)* Aa can feel it in me water!

MA':   What, fifteen bloody pounds, yer could feed the street for a month on that, yer bloody good for nothin waster, yer, an' where the Hell did yer get five pounds from, eh?

DA':   Don't be so bloody selfish, woman, *(Starts laughing)* yer talkin' beer an' fag money for six months with the winnin's! *(Goes into manic laughter)*

MA':   An' Aa hope yer bloody choke on it an' end

up in a gutter yer greedy-eyed bugger, Aa'll not come bloody lookin' for yer!

***

(Gosforth Park racing stadium. It's night time. The place is packed. The floodlights are on. We see the odds on the board. We see the Greyhounds in the traps, ready for the off. A murmur of excitement sweeps through the crowd, then a loud roar as the Hare goes whizzing on its' way. Then a hush, followed by a ear-bursting roar as the traps spring open. In a blur of limbs and technicolour, the pack explodes from the traps. In slow motion, Quassie tumbles out, the wrong way round, arse-first. We hear a big moan from the crowd. As Quassie does a backward roll, we see a close up of the lads' faces, stunned)

DAVY/SID: Jesus Christ, God Almighty!

(The crowd yell, scream and boo. Quassie, disorientated, does a couple of turns, finds his bearings, by which time the other Dogs are halfway around the track. Quassie finally takes up the chase. The crowd are still booing. Sid, in a shock stares into space and shakes his head from side to side)

DAVY: *(Trying to cheer Sid up)* Whey man Sid, just look at him go! C'mon Quassie Son, C'mon, ye show 'em!

(Quassie moves like lightning, inching up the pack with every stride)

DAVY: *(Turning to Sid, excitedly)* Yer were right Sid, man, he's like a friggin' rocket! Go on Quassie!

(Sid doesn't hear, he's miles away. We see Dogs racing in slow motion, we see Davy urging the Dog on, we see Sid looking heavenward, shaking his head from side to side, muttering)

"Aa held me breath, crossed me fingers an' prayed for a miracle, 'Please God, let all the other Dogs fall over'. Not much of a prayer Aa know, but it's all Aa could think of at the time. Aa didn't breathe

again 'til the race was over. The crowd, well, they screamed blue bloody murder. They were bayin' for blood, and Aa'm not sure, but Aa think the blood they wanted was wor Sids', mine and the Dogs. One thing was for certain tho', wor Sid never heard them, he was miles away. *(Sid has his mouth open, still gazing up at the stars)* **Well, he could have wished on every star in the sky that night, but it still wouldn't change the fact that Quassie was one of those Dogs that only comes 'round once in a lifetime, a freak of nature, the opposite way round t' every other Greyhoond. Maybe it was the shape of him, Aa don't know. Maybe his hump could have had somethin' t' do with it, interferin' with his centre of gravity an' balance an' all that. Anyway, there was no disputin' the fact that Quassie could do a bit of a Houdini, turnin' himsel' in the traps an' comin' out arse-first every time!"**

(On the second and last lap, Quassie manages to catch the tail end of the pack. The race ends, with Quassie coming in second from last. We then see Quassie jump the fence and wagging his tail, he trots towards the lads)

DAVY: *(Worried)* Bloody hell, Sid, don't look now but Quassie's just lobbed over the fence an' he's headin' this way!

(There is mass jeering, with shouts of 'Fix, fix', as the crowd grow nastier by the second)

SID: *(Shaking his head)* Why me, why bloody me? *(Then notices Dog)* Well Aa'll go t' bloody Hell! Aa think it's time we made ourselves scarce! Howay, run like mad!

(The lads look around, looking for an exit, then make a dash for it. Quassie follows loyally at their heels, still wagging his tail)

"Aa reckon that's the first time in our lives we'd actually agreed, an' definitely the first time we'd ever dodged out of the Dogs' instead of in!"

(We see the lads sneaking out, looking both ways, they run the first fifty yards, then they slow down, and with hands deep in pockets, heads down, they head for home at a slow walk. Quassie follows, still wagging his tail, tongue hanging out. It starts to rain)

***

(We see the lads, dejected, as they approach Byker Bridge. The Bridge is deserted. The rain has stopped, the sky is clear. They look up to the stars as they walk, with Quassie in tow. They stop and continue to gaze up at the stars)

SID: *(From the heart)* Did yer ever wish upon a star, Davy?

DAVY: What, yer takin' the piss tho', Sid?

SID: Naw, Aa'm serious, man, have yer?

DAVY: *(Thinks about it, shrugs shoulders)* Oh aye, many a time, but it never made a ha'pennies worth of difference, never ever changed. *(Laughs ironically, slaps Sid on the back)* In fact things got worse, it's like there's no bloody Santa Clause, *(Looks Sid in the eye)* can yer remember that? Yer told us that when Aa was only a bit of a bairn.

SID: *(Smiling)* Aye, it was for yer own good tho'!

DAVY: Oh aye, an' how d' yer make that out like?

SID: *(Sadly)* Aa didn't want yer t' build yer hopes up did Aa. We never got no toys, did we?

DAVY: Aye, but doesn't that only make yer wish all the more?

SID: True. *(A few seconds silence, Sid ruffles Davys' hair)* An' what d' yer wish for these days then?

DAVY:	If Aa told yer it'd never come true would it? But Aa'll tell yer anyway. There's this one wish Aa'm always wishin' for.
SID:	*(Happily surprised)* Getaway man, an' what's that like? Tell us, go on, what's it?
DAVY:	*(Takes a step back)* Calm down man, Aa'll tell yer what Aa really wish for, it's just that sometimes Aa really wish yer'd act yer bloody age, man, Sid!
SID:	*(Taken aback)* Who, me? *(On the defensive, reverting back to Bogarde)* An' what d'yer mean by that, kiddo?
DAVY:	*(Matter of factly)* That's exactly what Aa mean, ye an' yer Humphrey bloody Bogarde or John Wayne or Jimmy Cagney impersonations!
SID:	Oh aye, an' what d' yer bloody mean by that, like?
DAVY:	*(from the heart)* For Christs' sake, yer a bloody phoney, man. The trouble with ye is yer've seen too many pictures, yer live in one of them bloody fantasy worlds, Jesus Christ Sid, just be yersel' man, *(Joking)* an' talk proper like what Aa dee an' not like them bloody fictional Gangster or Cowboy hero's of yours all the time!
SID:	Oh aye, that's true, maybes Aa have seen too many pictures, but what's wrong with that like, so have ye!
DAVY:	Aye, but…

SID: Aye but nowt! An' what yer says about me bein' phoney an' livin' in a fantasy world an' that, speak for yersel'!

DAVY: Who me, what d' yer mean like?

SID: Ye know what Aa mean. Only last week yer rode home from the picture hoose on yer imaginary horse playin' Cowboys an' Injuns, slappin' yer arse an' shootin' everyone in sight with yer fingers an' lassoin' bloody lamposts with an invisible rope!

DAVY: Oh aye, playin', that's the difference, Aa'm only playin', the next day it's back t' reality for me! Back t' the real world, back t' planet Byker!

SID: Anyways, what's wrong with wantin' t' be like the stars on the big screen eh?

DAVY: *(With feeling, points to the heavens)* Them's the only stars yer can count on, Sid man! Just like Aa've been tellin' yer, the bloody film stars are all phoneys! They're not real Sid, they're only actors, bloody pretendin' t' be someone they're not!

SID: If that's the case then, what is real Davy, what is real?

DAVY: This is friggin' real, man, everythin' around us, look, this is life, *(Gestures with open hands)* Byker's not bloody Hollywood, but it sure is real, Sid, it sure is bloodywell real, it's all bricks an' mortar, a' we're the lifeblood of it. 'Never forget yer roots' me Granda' used t' say t' us when we was young uns, remember that? Sittin' in his rockin' chair with his woodbine hangin' off his bottom lip. *(Laughs)*

SID: Aye, an' where did the poor bugger end up? In a bloody wheelchair, crippled wi' hard graft, livin' in an old peoples' home bein' treat like shit an' gettin' fed on worse! If that's reality, Davy, yer can keep it! Aa'll tell yer somethin' for nowt tho, life's what yer make of it, it's up t' yersel' t' make an' take yer chances, well, isn't it?

DAVY: *(Not sure)* Is it? Well that depends on who yer listen t' Sid, me uncle Joe reckons life's a bitch an' then yer die!

SID: Aye maybe in the olden days when he was young, but not any more. Us, we can change it, we can make things happen, create our own opportunities!

DAVY: Aa don't get yer Sid, how's that, like? Creatin' opportunities, what d' yer mean?

SID: What Aa'm tryin' t' say is, 'Yer can be any bugger yer like!' *(Pointing to his head)* It's all in here, man, it's all in the mind.

DAVY: *(Shudders, pulls up his coat collar)* Hope yer right Sid, 'cos at the minute Aa feel like shit, Aa'm sick of me bloody life. Aa wish Aa was some bugger else, an' somewhere else, anywhere but here. Aa hate this bloody place, me, Aa hate school an' all, them bloody stuck-up teachers tellin' yer t' do what they want yer t' do an' not lettin' yer do what yer really want t' do, yer can't change that can yer?

SID:	An' that's how Aa used t' feel man, but not anymore, Aa'll show them, Aa'll show them all, just ye wait an' see!
DAVY:	Them? Who's them like?
SID:	Them who thinks they're better than us! What Aa'm tryin' t' say is, well, who knows who yer could be? Me, Aa reckon yer could be anybody yer want t' be an' do anythin' yer want if yer put yer mind t' it.
DAVY:	*(Lifting both arms in the air)* D' yer think Aa could fly then? Aa always wanted t' fly.
SID:	*(Smiling)* Oh aye, flyin's easy man, it's the landin' that's the problem. But yer've still got t' be realistic, don't reach for the sky. Like Aa says, it's all in the mind, just like in that picture.
DAVY:	There yer go again! Ye an' that bloody picture, that picture this, this picture that, what friggin' picture this time, man?
SID:	Just bide with us a minute man, remember 'The Wizard of Oz'?
DAVY:	Oh aye, now yer talkin', great picture that was!
SID:	Bloodywell was that an' all, now listen, this is what Aa'm gettin' at. Can yer remember what the Lion wanted?
DAVY:	*(Thinking)* What d'yer mean like?
SID:	For cryin' out loud, in the bloody picture man! The Lion, the Scarecrow an' the Tin man, they

was all lookin' for somethin' they wanted, aye, that's what they went t' Oz for, t' see that Wizard bloke, aye?

DAVY: Oh aye, that's right, Aa remember now!

SID: Well, then, can yer remember what it was the Lion was after?

DAVY: Er, aye, got it!

SID: Well?

DAVY: He was lookin' for some courage wasn't he, 'cos he was a coward an' he wanted t' be brave!

SID: Right, an' the Scarecrow, what'd he want?

DAVY: *(Laughing, and going into Scarecrow walk)* If Aa only had a brain Aa'd know that one!

SID: *(Laughing)* Ha ha, right again, an' what about...

DAVY: A heart, the Tin man wanted a heart didn't he!

SID: That's right, but the thing is, they already had what they were searchin' for, only they didn't know it! An' that owld fraud of a Wizard, he wasn't a Wizard at all! Even so, he gave them what they never had, an' yer know what that was?

DAVY: Aye, he gave the Lion a medal, the Tin man a watch an' the Scarecrow...

SID: Naw man, he gave them self-belief, that's what he gave them, yer've got t' believe in yersel'

	Davy lad, 'cos if yer don't believe in yersel', no bugger else is goin' t' believe in yer, are they?
DAVY:	Aye, but…
SID:	But what?
DAVY:	How the Hell can yer believe in yersel' Sid? Yer the biggest bullshitter in Byker bar me Fatha', yer'd say anythin' but yer prayers!
SID:	*(Shrugs and laughs)* That's not what Aa'm on about, what Aa'm sayin' is, er, er, how can Aa put it? Got it, life's just like the lyrics t' that song.
DAVY:	Eh, what song's that?
SID:	Yer know, the one that goes, 'Yer've got t' have a dream…'
DAVY:	Eh, what yer bloody on about? Aa haven't got a clue what yer mean!
SID:	*(Laughs)* Look kidda, we had a dream, we made a go of it, didn't we!
DAVY:	Aye an' we made a right Dogs arse of it an' all!
SID:	*(Laughing)* Ha ha, aye, we did that, but one of these days we'll show 'em!
DAVY:	Anyway, what d' yer bloody mean by 'we', eh?
SID:	*(With feeling)* You an' me kidda, that's who Aa mean, we're a team now, *(Big smile)* aye, we might have failed on our first money-makin'

quest, but there's always tomorrow, what d' yer say, *(Extending hand)*, let's shake on it, partner.

DAVY: Partner? Aa'm not yer friggin' partner, Aa'm yer Brotha'!

SID: *(Hugs Davy, John Wayne drawl)*, Yer better believe it, pardner, yer better believe it!

(Davy starts chuckling to himself, then laughs aloud)

SID: What's so funny, yer barmy sod!

DAVY: Oh nowt, it's just, well, Aa was thinkin', it could have been worse.

SID: An' how d' yer make that out? Were penniless, soaked t' the skin, knackered, clammin' with hunger an' proud bloody owners of a Racin' Dog that just so happens t' run out of the traps bloody arse first, an' yer says it could be worse! *(Laughs)* Bloody Laurel an' Hardy have better luck than this on a bad day, it could be worse, yer must be jokin'!

DAVY: *(Nodding his head)* Aye, just imagine if we'd have told the old man, an' knowin' him the greedy-eyed sod, he wouldn't have just put his shirt on, he'd have put his best Sunday suit on Quassies back an' all!

SID: *(Laughing)* Aye, Aa suppose yer right there Davy lad, mind yer, Aa nearly told him tho', Aa don't know why, wanted him t' be proud of us Aa s'pose.

DAVY: Him! Proud of us, yer must be mad! Pigs'll bloody fly an' all one day!

SID:	The thing that stopped us was he probably wouldn't have believed it, us havin' a record-breakin' Racin' Dog, the old sod never believed anythin' Aa ever told him.
DAVY:	Aye, me neither.
SID:	Aye, he only listens t' wor Tommy, with him bein' the youngest an' all. *(Laughs)* Imagine that, me Fatha', Bykers' big-time gamblin' man, puttin' his months beer an' tab money on a bloody Dog that runs backwards! *(Laughs)* He'd be bloody gutted, never live it down would he. It's a shame we never told him, eh! Do the bugger no harm t' get hammered off the bookies, serve the old bugger right!
DAVY:	*(Chuckling)* Well, yer never know, he might have got wind of it from a little bird.
SID:	What yer on about!
DAVY:	Well, Aa went an' told wor young un', Aa says, 'Listen Tommy, whatever yer do, don't tell me Da' about how fast the Dog is!' An' well, yer know yersel' how good Tommy is when it comes t' keepin' secrets!
SID:	Aye, it'd serve the silly old sod right if he'd found out an' put money on it, he'll never bloody learn. He'd bet on a one-legged man in an arse-kickin' contest if the odds were right!!
DAVY:	*(Laughing)* An' Aa wouldn't care tho', but he's the worst loser in the world an' all!
SID:	Boy, yer can say that again, he's a bloody lunatic

if his bets don't come in. Still, Aa'd love t' see his face if he'd put money on wor Flash! Can yer imagine that, Davy?

DAVY: *(Laughs)* Aye, it's not over hard t' imagine, Aa don't think he'd take it too gracefully!

(Both lads start laughing)

***

(We see Da' banging his head, and thumping his fists against the living room wall. He swears in rhythm)

DA': Bastard, bastard, bastard, bastard...

(We see Ma' in the kitchen, giggling to herself)

Ma': Would yer like a nice pot of tea, darlin', *(Laughs aloud)* Aa wouldn't bet on it!

DA': ...bastard, bastard, bastard.

***

(Back to the lads, they're both still laughing aloud. Sid extends his hand again)

SID: Partners?

DAVY: *(Shaking on it)* Partners!

(We see the lads shake hands, hug each other in a show of affection, then start sparring for fun. After a few combinations, the lads move apart and raise their hands above their heads like champions winning a bout. They stop, panting for breath as they gaze up at the stars)

"We wished on the biggest star in the sky that night, then changed

our minds an' wished on the moon. A little chill ran up me spine an' a wonderful feelin' took possession of me body an' soul, Aa never wanted that moment t' end."

THE LADS:	*(Sing together)* SOMEWHERE, OVER THE RAINBOW, WAY UP HIGH, THERE'S A LAND THAT AA'VE HEARD OF, ONCE IN A LULLABY...
DAVY:	*(John Wayne drawl)* By the way, pardner, this town ain't big enough for the three of us, what we gonna do with the Goddam, good for nuttin' mutt?
SID:	*(Laughs, looks down at Quassie)* He never did answer to Flash, did he?
DAVY:	Nor Lassie, either.
THE LADS:	*(Sing)* ...WHERE TROUBLES MELT LIKE LEMON DROPS AWAY UP IN THE CHIMNEY TOPS, THAT'S WHERE YER'LL FIND ME...'

(The lads stop and lean on the handrail and look thoughtfully down into the Ouseburn far below)

SID:	*(Quassie Modo impression)* Esmerelda, Aa says we throw the humpy-backed freak over the bridge an' back int' the sewers it crawled out of!
DAVY:	*(In a womans voice, goes onto all fours)* Oh no, don't be so cruel, Quassie darlin', *(He starts to scuttle backwards)* Aa says we just run away from the poor creature!

(Both lads start laughing until there are tears on both their faces. Quassie sits

there, wagging his tail, tongue hanging out, almost laughing with them. Both lads are now on their haunches and hug and stroke the Dog at the same time. Quassie responds by licking the lads' faces and wagging his whole backend)

DAVY: Yer a good boy, what are yer? Yer a canny lad!

SID: Yer are that, son"! Yer a bloody champion Quassie, wor bloody champion, an' don't let anyone tell yer different!

DAVY: Oh aye, he is that alright, 'Quassie, the Byker Flash!'

(General laughter, the lads do a little jig, the Dog joins in. Then they slowly go on their way, the Dog close at their heels. They sing aloud, the Dog howls with them, as they finish their song through tears of happiness and joy)

LADS: ...SOME...WHERE, OVER THE RAINBOW, BLUEBIRDS FLY, BIRDS FLY OVER THE RAINBOW, OH WHY...OH WHY, CAN'T I...

"We patterned our lives after our idols on the silver screen. Those larger than life stars got inside our heads, makin' us who we thought we wanted t' be...

(We see the lads from behind, arms around each others' shoulders, slowly walk into the distance, Quassie still at their sides)

...And later, much later, after all the beer we'd drank t'gether t' try an' forget them, but we never could an' never would, we've finally realised they'll be part of us for ever...

(They are almost over the bridge)

...For better or for worse...

(FREEZE-FRAME. The moon shines on the wet grey cobbles, reflecting a golden, yellow brick road)

...they helped make us what we are!"

(Judy Garland picks up the song)

The End

"Wor War"

By Mark James

CHARACTERS

MA, in her thirties.

GRANDA, in his sixties.

BETTY, 13 their eldest daughter.

MARKY, 10 their eldest son.

UNCLE JOE, in his forties.

AUNTY LIZZIE, in their forties.

Mrs HEDLEY, in her thirties.

AMY HEDLEY, 18 The Hedley's eldest daughter.

SCENE 1: UPSTAIRS ANCIENT FLAT – LIVING ROOM – TIME DURING WWII

(Off Stage: The Houses are tumbledown soot-blackened, back to back, terraces. A tiny scullery leads to a rickety worn out flight of stairs. Down the stairs is the outside netty located in the back yard.
Through the back gate, a cobbled stone lane.
Situated in the lane stands the Communal air raid shelter.)

VERA LYNN *(Sings)* – "There'll be Blue Birds over the White Cliffs of Dover"

NARRATOR – "The lovely voice of Vera Lynn singing an Old familiar song takes me back........."

SONG ENDS – "Tomorrow, just you wait and see."

(Ma, Granda, Betty & Marky sit huddled around the wireless)

A VOICE ON THE WIRELESS IS SAYING – "This Country is now at War with Germany."

NARRATOR – "Me Scared, NAW!...I was too young and daft to be scared. An excitement ran through me from Head to Toe."

GRANDA – *(with contempt)* "Bloody Gormans..Hu! nowt ever changes."

MA – *(Looking Heavenward)* "Jesus, God help us."

GRANDA – "Aye, it's a Bloody Miracle. We'll all be wantin' before this little lot is over.........A'm tellin' yer!!"

BETTY – "Should I pray to God Ma..........Should I"..............

MA – *(Hugging Betty)* "Aye you do that Pet and don't you worry love ....God will keep us safe and sound"

BETTY –– *(On her Knees Praying)* "Our Father which art in Heaven"............

MARK – *(To Audience)* "Oh no he's not, he's in the Boozer isn't he!"

MA – *(Singing)* "Bless this House".....

NARRATOR – "The bombs didn't drop right away like we thought they would. We waited for the Bombers to come....just like we knew they would."

....

SCENE 2: SAME LIVING ROOM.
MA SITS KNITTING, GRANDA READS THE PAPER, BETTY NURSES THE BABY, MARKY LOOKS OUT OF THE WINDOW. IT'S DARK OUTSIDE

GRANDA – *(Reading from paper)* "Them poor buggas' down South is havin' it rough. Listen to this – One Fella says that just as he grasped his front door handle, a bloody great bomb fell and blew his hoose oot of 'ees hand......................whey yer bugga, fancy that!!"

MA – "Will you shut up You're frightening the Bairns."

GRANDA – "An' anotha Fella reckons a bomb blast stripped him naked – (looks up from paper) – Jenny love, Aa reckon ah should start warmin' me long John's just in case.

MA – "Oh aye, we'll all be blown to hell, an there's that silly owld sod worrying aboot showin' his bare arse – anyway, will yer stop reading that bloody paper!"

GRANDA – (Smiling to Himself reads from the paper) "An' can yer believe this: That same fellas wife was sucked up the chimney an' he's not seen hide nor hair of her since."

MA – "Fatha, ye talk a load of old rubbish..you do!!"

(A siren wails – Baby cries)

MA – "Noisy buggas, that's the tenth time this week that they've woke the Bairn up."

GRANDA – "Take nee notice Pet, they're only trying them oot."

BETTY – "The Bairn can wear me lug plugs an' gas mask."

MA – "Divin't yee worry aboot the Bairn love. It does them the world of good ti cry."

(The siren still wails).

BETTY – *(Concerned)* – "Them sirens is gannin' on for ages the nite Ma."

GRANDA – "You take no notice Pet, it'll be just another false alarm. *(He Grins & Jokes)* "It's probably Henry Headley's pigeons comin' home to roost.

MARKY – "Don't 'em birds know there's a bloody war on."

GRANDA – "Naw, but they'll soon find oot, when me 'n' Henry wring their necks an' they end up in a pigeon pie."

MA – *(Concerned)* – "Aa think we'd better gan doon the shelter Dad. Better safe than sorry."

GRANDA – "Had-a-way to Hell woman. Them bloody air raid shelters is a bloody waste of time if you ask me."

MA – *(Annoyed)* – "Nee bugga's askin' Yee. You awkward owld Sod."

(Betty & Mark at window)

BETTY – "Ma, all the sky's lit up. The Search lights is on."

MARKY – *(Excited)* – "Flippin' heck man.......yi can see 'em as plain as day!! Big and Grey...can even make out the markings on their wings."

GRANDA – *(Chuffed)* – "Well I telt yer didn't Aa...........Henry Hedleys bloody pigeons."

MARKY – *(Sarcastic)* – "Nah Granda................Adolf Hitlers Bombers."

GRANDA – *(Shocked)* – "Well I'll gan ti Hell."

MA – "There's nee arguing with that."

(**UNCLE JOE** *(Air Raid Warden) voice comes from off stage)*

UNCLE JOE – "Hurry yersel's up now. Cum' on..Cum' on. Everyone to the shelters at the double. The Gormons is cummin'."

*(***PAUSE** – *Then the drone of the bombers overhead)*

UNCLE JOE – "Me, Aa stand corrected them durty bugga's is already here."

(Panic Stations as Ma dishes out orders)

MA – "You's two come away from that winda quickly. Betty yee put oot the Gas light. Wor Marky, pull the black – oot doon."

(Ma grabs hold of the Baby)

BETTY – "Me, I've got the candles Ma."

MA – "Good Lass. Quick grab hold of them blankets wor Marky."

(Marky is still peeping out of the window)

MA – *(Shouts)* – "Marky, Marky were the Hell are yer. I'm warnin' yer, if You don't come away from that window quick. I'll put me foot up yer arse!!"

(They come together ready to move off)

GRANDA – "Diven't panic, keep calm, keep calm. Single file doon the stairs (jokes) I'll take the lead if yee gan first."

(As they leave the Stage, Betty runs back & disappears from view)

MA – *(Shouts)* – "Betty, Me Bairn, whee are yer gannin'."

(Betty arrives back on Stage carrying a cardboard box)

BETTY – *(Panting)* – "The kittens Ma, We nearly forgot the Kittens. *(Pulls a sad Face)*......but Aa cannit find Winston."

MA – "Bugga Winston, cats have got nine lives.....Old Winston wi'nnit miss one of them."

(As they walk off, Granda hesitates)

GRANDA – *(Panicking)* – "Had on a minute."

MA – "For Gods sake man...what is it now!!"

GRANDA – "Me teeth....Aav forgot me false teeth."

MA – *(Loud & Clear)* – "What Yi want with Yer false teeth yer silly owld Bugga, they're droppin' bombs.......not bloody mince pies."

(In step, they mark time on the stage, Marky & Betty sing)

MARKY & BETTY – "Hitler has only got one ball. The other is in the Albert Hall"....................

MA, GRANDA, MARKY & BETTY – "Himmler has something similar, and Old Goerbel's has no balls at all."

(They march from the stage in step)

....

SCENE 3: AIR RAID SHELTER. EVERYONE IS SINGING – "LILLY MARLENE".

(**UNCLE JOE** *(Air Warden) Full of self importance, dishes out orders)*

UNCLE JOE – "Hello, hello, hello Ladies and Gentlemen."

GRANDA – *(Points to Lizzy)* – "She ain't no Lady, She's Your Lass."

UNCLE JOE – "Cheer up Mrs Headley, it may never happen."

(Granda looks at Amy Headleys' Belly)

GRANDA – *(Sarcastic)* – "By the looks of Her, it already has."

MRS HEADLEY – *(Defensive)* – "I'd like you to know that our Amy is a good Lass. Ain't yer Love."

GRANDA – "Aye, good for nowt."

MRS HEADLEY – *(Proud)* -- "Grand news everybody, Wor Amy is engaged to be Wed."

MA – "Congratulations Mrs Headley................anyone we know."

MRS HEADLEY – *(Poshlike)* – "Know.....No Mrs James He ain't from around here *(to Amy)*...is he my dear."

AMY – *(Very Broad)* – "Na ,, ee's not from around here, ee's not..."

(we hear bombs in the distance)

UNCLE JOE – "If it's the shipyards they're after, they're way off bloody target."

MARKY – "Lord Haw Haw reckons the Gormans is gonna bomb Gatesheed with bars of soap..........i hope they bomb us with bars of chocolate."

UNCLE JOE – "That's the spirit, keep yer chin up son. How does that song go again.." "Oh Oh Oh, the buzzin' of the bees"..........

(**UNCLE JOE** *Sings "Big Rock Candy Mountain"*)

AUNT LIZZIE – *(Proud)* – "Ain't My Joe great...don't he raise to the occasion."

MA – "So does hot air."

AUNT LIZZIE – "You would'nt think it but this time last week he was a checky in The Bambrough Picture Hall."

MA – "Aye nowt changed. Joe's still flashin' his torch in the dark."

MA – *(To Joe)* – "When does the big picture start."

UNCLE JOE – "Well now everybody settle, it'll soon be over."

GRANDA – *(Laughs)* – "Ha!, that's what they says about the last one."

MA – *(To Granda)* – "Miserable owld Bugga."

UNCLE JOE – "Well, I must love you's & leave you's, now duty calls. Tara for now then.........i'll keep you informed."

(Joe comes to attention, salutes & marches proudly away. Turns his head to Lizzy, Lizzy waves.)

UNCLE JOE – *(Sings)* – "Wish me luck as you wave me Goodbye"............

AUNT LIZZY – *(Proud)* – "Ain't my Joe handsome in his uniform."

MRS HEADLEY – *(Sarcastic)* – "You call a tin hat and armband a uniform. Our Amy's Fiance is a Yank. You's should see him............now that's what I call a uniform."

GRANDA – *(Sarcastic)* – "Yankee Bloody Doodle – Dandy."

AMY – *(Proud)* – "Aye, an' my frankie's gorra chest full of medals in' all."

GRANDA – *(Laughs)* – "Ha! Chest full of medals...don't make me laugh. They get a medal if they can wipe their own arse."

AMY – *(in defence)* – "I'd like you to know My Frankie is a real Hero."

GRANDA – "Oh aye, he must be to gan oot with Yee....*(To audience)*... Her face would frighten the Vulture's off a deed Donkey."

MA – *(To Granda)* – "Now there's no need to get personal Dad. Apologise to the Lass."

GRANDA – *(Sarcastic)* – "Sorry Love, You cannit help takin' after yer Mutha."

MRS HEADLEY – "You take no notice love. They're only jealous."

AMY – "Aye that's right Ma......they'll be laughin' on the other side of their faces when 'am Wed an' livin' in Hollywood, the good old U.S. of A."

MARKY – *(Excited)* – "Is he a cowboy."

AMY – "Eeeee, aye. He's got this own ranch. But how did Yer guess."

GRANDA – "They're all bloody cowboys, aren't they. An' I'll tell Yer summit for nowt. The day your Yank Marries you,...is the day I'll show me arse in Fenwick's shop window."

MA – *(To Granda)* – "Divin't be such a grumpy owld sod. Let the lass have her dreams........it does nee harm to dream."

GRANDA – *(Sad)* – "Sorry, but it's just I don't wanna build up the Lassie's hope up.......that's all."

MA – "Aye, but the way things is gannin, we all need a bit of hope."

(**MA** *sings "Keep the home Fires Burning"....everyone joins in. As the song ends we hear the drone of the bombers directly overhead.*)

GRANDA – *(Ironic)* – "Divin't wanna spoil the party but here come the bugga's again."

....

(We hear a loud BOOM!!)

AUNT LIZZIE – "By Christ, that one was close."

MRS HEADLEY – "Keep yer backs off the wall."

BETTY – "Why's that like"....

MRS HEADLEY – "'Cause they reckon them vibrations will weaken your spine."

GRANDA – *(Nods at Amy)* – "Too late for her then."

AMY – *(Innocent)* – "Funny you should say that, me back's killin' us."

(Uncle Joe pops his head around the door entrance)

UNCLE JOE – "Bad news I'm afraid, Newbridge Street is takin' a reel hammerin'..........the goods station has went up in flames. Makes you wonder how they knew exactly where ti drop the bombs."

GRANDA – "Don't take a bloody genius to figure that one out. The buggas built it."

MA – "Whey.......yer bugga.......Really?"

GRANDA – "Aye, Jerry built it........it was."

NARRATOR – "On that night 28 aircraft attacked. Locally 57 people were killed, 100 houses were destroyed and about 1000 people made homeless."

UNCLE JOE – "The sky is bright Red owa Manor's Station way"...

MRS HEADLEY – "It'll be with all that butter and sugar."

MA – "What a waste.....eh!"

(We hear a loud bang.....Everyone jumps.)

MA – *(Hand on Heart)* – "God help us."

GRANDA – *(To Audience)* – "ME, Aa was in the last War, an' I'll tell yer something for nowt. There's definitely nee bloody God."

(Pause)

(Uncle Joe Pops his head around the entrance door.)

UNCLE JOE – "Hello, hello, hello.....do you's want to hear the good news first or the bad?"

BETTY – *(Worried)* – "Tell us the bad news first Uncle Joe.....please."

UNCLE JOE – "Well the bad news is, can yer believe.....A greet big woppa of a bomb has dropped on St. Lawrences Church doon owa Lane."

MRS HEADLEY – "That's terrible bad news."

MA – "Aa call's it good news......we're lucky to be alive.....well aren't we."

MRS HEADLEY – *(Crosses Herself)* – "My God Jenny, you're right 'n all."

(Aunt Lizzy gives Granda a dirty look)

AUNT LIZZIE – *(Saintly)* – "Goes to show, it's true what they say, God looks after his own."

GRANDA – *(Sarcastic)* – "Aa think you mean the Devil pet................ anyway Joe, what's the good news?"

AUNT LIZZIE – "Just being alive has got to be the good news, well hasn't it."

UNCLE JOE – "True, but what I was goin' to say is.............the good news is...............the bomb didn't gan off."

(Pause)

UNCLE JOE – "An' take it from me the blast would'ave flattened the whole Street."

(Granda looks to above and talks to God)

GRANDA – "Better late than never.....I suppose."

(Everyone says "The Lords Prayer")

NARRATOR – "On the 7th of May 1945, Germany surrendered."

GRANDA – *(To audience)* – "Aye, we showed 'em....they don't call us the Bulldog Breed for nowt"...*(he waves a fist at the crowd)*

NARRATOR – "A lot of people in spite of all the fear, the loss and the suffering will tell you".............

MA – *(To Audience)* – "Aye, although we didn't know it at the time. Them war years was the happiest of our lives."

NARRATOR – "Their lasting memory is funnily enough, not of the fear, food rationing, blackouts and bombs"................

MARKY – *(To Audience)* – "The memory is of what grand people we all were then. And I was so proud of me Ma."

MA – *(To Audience)* – "Oh Aye, it's something you'll never ever forget......it was just great to be alive."

MRS HEADLEY – *(To Audience)* – "It was great seeing people come together like that. People were much nicer then. An' wor Amy, she married her Yank."

AMY – *(To Audience in an American accent)* – "Yeah, Folks, yer bet yer sweet life I did."

NARRATOR – "It was a great Community spirit. I wouldn't have missed it for the World. We were the lucky ones."

....

SCENE 5: BACK LANE – FLAGS & DECORATIONS OUT, VICTORY SIGNS PAINTED AND CHALKED ON THE WALLS & DOORS' EVERYONE IS DANCING THE CONGA, UP & DOWN THE LANE. DAD, BACK FROM THE WAR, STILL IN UNIFORM, TAKES THE LEAD......................They Dance off

stage & return to sing "England's, Green and Pleasant Land."

NARRATOR – "The V – For Victory signs that had been painted and chalked on the walls for four years had at last been fulfilled."

MA – (To Audience) – "The ships on the Tyne gave three short blasts on their sirens and one long one. The morse code for Owld Mr Churchill's V-sign for Victory."

MARKY – *(To Audience)* – "And me Granda…God Bless Him, showed his bare arse in Fenwick's shop window."

(Pause)

(Vera Lynn sings "There'll be Blue Birds Over The White Cliffs of Dover")

NARRATOR – "It's the lovely voice of Vera Lynn, that takes me back."

THE END

"Memories"

By Mark James

"Yesterday's Song."

I'm getting on a bit, can't argue with that.

These days I spend most of my time dreaming of the past, I felt so alive then. Now I seem almost half dead at times...and seem to die a little with each passing day.

Love to walk....It helps keep me alive and tickin'.

Must have a million tunes stored away in me head and every one of them comes with it's own memory.

My feet have a mind of their own and they take me wherever my mood wants to go.

Today the sun is shining, I feel almost young again, ain't life grand!!

As I walk the rhythms from the past go merrily bouncing along in my head. The years melt away.

I'm just a kid again and I'm late for school again......................

With a hop – an – a – skip, I almost break into an arthritic run.

A classroom window is wide open, can hear the kids singing...

"ALL THINGS BRIGHT AND BEAUTIFUL...."

The song takes me way back to a time when one of those wonderful young voices was mine....

Old Byker seemed like a black and white world. A square mile of belching chimney's and back to back, row after row of soot blackened tumbledown houses.

Everyone had nowt. Times were hard. Me mother and me fatha were hard as nails...the poor buggas had to be!!

Maybe that's why there were no kisses or cuddles in our house...not even a kind word!!

I used to envy the ragman's horse....he had a better life than me.

You had to laugh at life.

Even so, there were times when life laughed at me –

Raggy-arsed, hands deep in pockets, head down...

I wandered the streets of Byker like a lost soul....

What I was looking for God only knows....

....

The sun shone behind him as he entered the classroom and the dazzling light played tricks with me eyes.

A halo reflected from golden bryl-creamed glistening hair...he seemed to hover, like a vision in a blinding glow.

"Good morning boys." He introduced himself, with a nod and a wink.

"I'm your new music teacher. My name is ...."
....and he paused like a comedian when reading his punch line...
"Mr Angel....I'm from Heaven –on Tyne!!"

We all laughed...but he wasn't joking he really was...
Mr Angel, from Hebburn – on – Tyne.
His blue eyes sparkled, then glowed as if he could look right inside me and
see everything I am, ever was or would ever be.
And for the blink of an eye, I'd have sworn he had wings.................?

Could have told him for nowt, he was definitely flogging a dead horse.
The music class, just like the art class, had always been a bit of a joke.
No one had ever taken them serious. Weren't we supposed to be the hard
lads. Even so, I daren't admit it but I was quite looking forward to the
music lesson.

....

"Righty Oh.." he almost sang...flashing a smile that showed straight-even
pearly white teeth set in a handsome face.
"I want you all just to relax and listen....most important use your
imagination."
Then he paused for effect, then stated –
"People get what they imagine."

It was awfully hard to imagine that..........and I had to laugh 'cause – Me,
I lived in an imaginary world...a cartoon world inside my head!!

"Now is everyone settled." He asked.
Noses sniffled...throats coughed...Then silence.
A tuning – fork magically appeared in his hand. He held it like a magic
wand.
"**Doe**..." He sang and twanged the tuning – fork on his desk.
We sat hypnotised....staring at the vibrating fork.
The high-pitched eerie sound held us spellbound.
Taking us on a trip to an imaginary world....a magical carpet ride of
boyhood dreams....
Before us stood Henry V...clad in full armour....
We all recognised him immediately....we'd seen the film.

123

Henry grinned an evil grin and drew his mighty broadsword...ready for action.

"**Ray**..." He yelled his war – cry echoed around Agincourt Battlefield.
"**Ray**..." We answered in harmony and raised our swords...that only moments ago were 12" Rulers....
"**Me**..." Our Leader yelled and mounted his huge warhorse...
"**Far**..." Our warrior King sang and saluted us...his brave fighting men.....
"**So...**" He raised his mighty sword above his head and led us into battle...
"**La**..." Charge...into the breach we go.....
"**Te**..." ...For Saint George......
"**Doe**..." ......For Harry and for England....!!!!

The sound of the ragman's battered old bugle played out a tune...breaking the spell.
"Amazing..?" Said Mr Angel.
"Who's 'Arry?" I asked.
"Harry Blackbarry.." Answered Blacky....
"And we all knaa what he did...don't we? He shit in the Quarry!!"
I nodded me head, but was non the wiser.

....

The Gramaphone's windy-up handle creaked in agony as little Georgie Scott gave it all he got.
Chubby Harrison held his breath as he gently lifted and cocked the Silver chrome arm. Chubby looked in wonder as the record began to turn. He hesitated before he brought the arm down in slow motion.
"Phew...!!" he breathed a sigh of relief...when with a wobble and a jump the needle found the groove.
The music didn't come right away. At first there was a kind of crackling, scratching sound. We all laughed, 'cause Chubby thought that he'd broke it. When it did come, the music took us totally by surprise!!
We sat spellbound....as a cascade of wonderful sound exploded from another world into ours....
The music grabbed hold of my body and soul.
A tingling feeling ran up the back of my neck and buzzed around in me head. Leaving my body way behind....my mind went on a magical carpet ride to other times and places.

Fingals Cave – I could smell the salty sea and hear the waves crashing.

Morning – I could see the dawn sky...curtained with fringes of red and hear the Lark singing with joy to the new born day.

Moonlight Sinatra – I could almost touch the Stars.

It's funny how sweet and sentimental music can make the hardest of men cry.
I could have cried.....to tell you the truth I did!!

> Me....I had been more of a *"Leaning on the Lamppost..."*
> George Formby kinda Fella.

Classical music had been totally Alien...something to scoff at!!
That's what I was told....and that's what I believed.
So why was it long after the lesson had ended, the music stayed in my head.
I daren't mention it at home....me life wouldn't have been worth living.
Arty Farty was worse than a swearword in our house.

Nowt had really changed and yet I felt feelings I'd never felt before.
I wondered why I could feel them now??

As if by magic, my black and white world had transformed into a glorious Technicolor.....or was it that I looked at the world in a different light.
I was glad to be alive...and it showed.
Everywhere I went I whistled and hummed...
On the park I sang at the top of me voice.....on the netty I sang sweet and low...
Me Motha, always said I'd a bigger mouth than Tynemouth.
It proved to be right....when my high note bounced off the back yard wall and echoed down our lane amplifying the sound.
Windows vibrated, gas mantles exploded and me Granny's false teeth rattled in the glass.
It's funny how only a short time ago I was a daft lad who couldn't even shout "Coal.".....
Now, here I was, singing –
"My Love is Like a Red Red Rose" ....so sweet, you could almost smell them...

The music class went from strength to strength...
Names of new Heroes were heard around the playground...Elgar, Tchaikovsky and Mozart.

For a short while Football played second fiddle. Overnight, kids started singing that had never sang before...as if they had just found their voices. Where they really lost...or was it the first time in our lives that we had something to sing about!!

Blackie The Byker Basher decided to have his own theme song.....what was good enough for The Lone Ranger...................was good enough for Him...!!
-Blackie would sing... *"Swing Low Sweet Chariot..."* Just before he was gonna kick you in the Goolies.....

Stinker Brown...who had an awful habit of breaking wind...............
Sang *"Blow The Wind Southerly."*

Snotty Scotty sang, *"Green Sleeves."*

And me.........I sang – *"Oh for the wings of a Swallow."* ....but improvised with the words...
"And the arse of a dirty Crow...I'd fly to the top of a mou-n-tain and shite on the people be-lo-oow...........!!"
The words weren't important with a tune in me head...it was only natural –

You just had to sing............well didn't Yer..!!!

The first time Mr Angel tried to get us to sing in Harmony, it was a bit like asking different song-birds to sing the same song.
We sounded like cats being put through the mangle. It would take a miracle to get us to sing together...but then again, Mr Angel had a habit of turning the water from the Tyne...into wine!!

"Sing like that on the big day.." Mr Angel said glowing with pride.

It was our last rehearsal.

"And you will definitely win First Prize.." That was tomorrow and the Prize, a huge Silver trophy.

Every year, Choirs from all over the North East met in fierce Competition at The City Hall....all the posh Schools would be there.

Had to laugh when he said.. "Wear your best clothes boy's!!"

...as I stood in the only clothes I had.

For the first time in me life, I wore a tie...I'd borrowed it from Cousin Jim.

It was bright Yellow with hand painted fox and Hounds.

It looked great...until me Motha washed it...the paint ran...so did the Fox and hounds.

Boots spit-an-polished, faces scrubbed clean...and hair stuck down with Vaseline. Chest out, arms swinging...all in step, like troops into battle, we marched proudly over Byker Bridge.

The City Hall stood majestic...like an Ancient Greek Temple.

We felt like an invading horde of Barbarians.

The Hall was enormous...it smelt sweet and clean...of disinfectant.

We brought the smell of Muck, Sweat and Coal dust...the aroma of Byker through the doors!!

The place was packed out, mostly young girls...I wondered if they could smell us?...I could smell them.

A lovely looking Girl gave me a smile and I dropped stone cold dead... with an arrow through me heart. I tried to speak but nowt came out. She gave me a look that said I wasn't right in the head.

To tell you the truth, she wasn't much to look at but she was the first real lass to look at me.

The waiting was the worst...a river of sweat ran down the narrow of me back...my imagination ran away...with me in tow!!

We were surrounded by hostile savages screaming for our blood. It looked like a fight to the death.

We'd not leave this Hellhole alive...and I was desperate for the toilet!!

-          "And last but not leath'ed.." Announced a sour faced woman who
couldn't pronounce her esses...
"Waby Thr'eet Th'econdary..Modern Th'chool for bóy'th"...

That was when Cousin Jim's yellow tie threatened to choke us!!

The long march to the stage was a nightmare of a trudge. Through the mud, blood and bullets...we went like lambs to the slaughter. There was no turning back.
The deadly rat-tat-tat of the machine guns – cut us to pieces.
Barbwire ripped and tore us to shreds.
We followed our immortal leader....the bravest of the brave.
Finally our Band of Brothers...heroes one and all, reached our destiny... the centre of the stage.

"Waby Thr'eet Th'chool" The Woman announced.
"Will th'ing.." ......and she cringed.
"Jeruth'alem." She almost whispered...as if afraid to be heard.
She gave us a scornful look...then nodded, a righteous little nod to the audience, before leaving the stage.

Mr Angel stood like a gunfighter...his index finger pointed at us, loaded and cocked.
So it was either sing or be shot!!...
"Ready Boys?"..He asked...
We coughed and cleared our throats...Blackie adjusted his private parts... and on cue Stinker farted.
"All together boys." He said, and his hands began to move smooth...like ripples on a pond.
We took a deep breath, and started to sing –
"AND DID THOSE FEET IN ANCIENT TIMES..."
Mr Angel threw his weight from one foot to the other.......while his hands moved in wonderful gestures.....grasping and holding the tempo.
We sang with such feeling.....as we were swept along the crest of a wave.

As we came to the finale.......Mr Angel stood before us, his arms spread out wide like Jesus bestowing a Holy Sacrament.....
"I WILL NOT CEASE FROM MENTAL FLIGHT...."

We sang like disciples....to our Messiah.
Fingers clutching upwards, Mr Angel reached for the Sky.
His energy radiated...we bathed in it's glow as we sang...
"'TIL WE HAVE BUILT JERUSALEM.."

We shuddered with pure ecstasy and sang with all our hearts...
"IN ENGLANDS GREEN AND PLEASANT LAND.."

Mr Angels eye's sparkled...then glowed....then he exploded with a blinding
flash of pure energy and like a comet, he took off.......taking us with him,
body and soul.
Under the Rainbow and over the Moon...on a Rocket ship called
Imagination.......we headed for the Stars.

....

I can remember him telling us for no particular reason..." Death and Birth
are very much the same...they pass each other along the way."
It didn't make any sense at the time.
Death was still a stranger to us...and Birth still a mystery.
They reckon he knew all along that he wasn't long for this world...in fact,
he was living on borrowed time.
If that's the case, in a way I'm glad he went out in a blaze of glory.

When you think, he couldn't have had a better send off...even if he had
planned it himself. Between you and me, I think he did...right down to
the last detail –
We were very proud to be asked to sing at his funeral...and can you believe
it, he'd actually made the arrangements.

The Church was full...all posh and well to do...apart from us!!
"ALL THINGS BRIGHT AND BEAUTIFUL..." We sang!!
It was hard not to laugh...we were about as bright as a dark night...and if
our faces were our fortune, we'd die with hunger!!
Even so, we sang like angels and so sweet did we sing that by the end of
the song....everyone cried and wanted to believe in God.

....

Me voice broke overnight and so did me heart.

I'd gone to bed with the voice of a Skylark and woke up sounding like a Bullfrog down a well....!!

I left school and went straight into a life of hard graft.

I remember the ragman's Horse's lips curling up and he'd laugh at me coming down our lane back from work....knackered and covered in crap. He had a good right to laughin' an' all........nowt had changed, he still had a better life than me........and my job would kill a horse!! – It's a bloody miracle how it didn't kill me. –

These days, I still kid myself, I can sing...but wor lass. God bless her, tell's the truth....

She reckons – I'm the best..worst singer in the world.

Mind you, If I say so myself, I do a pretty good – *"Old Man River."*

If there is a God...and I would like to believe there is.............Mr Angel certainly was the answer to my prayers.

Maybe he really was my Guardian Angel.............Nah!!, I've had too many knocks on the head...I'm talking daft!!

Anyway, I can honestly say with hand on heart...and this is no word of a lie!!

Me...I don't believe in Angels...Cross me heart...cross me fingers and hope to die.

Funny how when I hear little kids singing –

"ALL THINGS WISE AND WONDERFUL...THE LORD GOD MADE THEM ALL.." ....Never fails to make me cry.

"Under the Rainbow and over the Moon. . . .
On a rocket ship called imagination. . .
We headed for the stars. ."

The End

"Last Bat"

"Haircuts really did hurt"

"Last Bat."

People passing in the street were giving me those funny looks again.
Maybe she had forgotten....I'd like to think she had and I certainly wasn't
going to remind her.
It was well past the time for my six monthly visit to the Barbers.

Anyway, I hated the dreaded Barbers and if I had my own way I'd never
have another hair cut...never again.
Could you believe that hair cuts could be painful? Besides, I was quite
pleased with my cave-man mop style.
There was something kind of sad at the thought of losing it.....the style
had grown on me, in more ways than one.

It wasn't just a head of hair...It was much more than that.
A curtain like fringe covered most of my face and hung down by my neck,
curling over my collar. I felt safe and snug inside my helmet of hair.
Most importantly of all, it concealed my identity, I could hide behind a
mask....of hair.
I could be anybody I wanted to be....all I had to do was use my
imagination.
I imagine myself in a Circus Sideshow...." The Wild Man of Borneo".
I would practice my Wild Man snarl and growl....looking at that thick
skeletal boy in the mirror.
I would flex my muscles....willing them to grow.
I would dream of a physique sculptured out of bronze.

My Dad quickly burst the Wild Man day dream...
"Get your bloody hair cut Wor Marky...you look like a big soft Girl."
He shouted at me from across the street on his way home from work.

I heeded his call and kept well out of his way.
At home I wet my hair under the cold tap and patted it down to try and
make it look presentable.

All that week and well into the next nothing was mentioned about haircuts
or the dreaded visit to the barbers. I thought to myself that the trick was
to get past Friday and I was safe for another week.

You see, Friday Afternoons were half price for kids and pensioners....there was no chance of my Mother paying full-price.

Anyway, there was me....creeping down the back stairway humming to myself....when "Gotcha!!"....A powerful hand grabbed me by the hair. It was me Mother.

"You my Lad are going straight to the Barbers after school." She yelled....pushing a sixpence into the palm of my hand.
"But Mam...." I almost begged......" The Winter is coming....brrrr!!"
I gave out an animated shiver....and pleaded," Let's wait until Spring?"
"Spring...." She shouted...." Don't be so daft....I'll give you Spring."
And clipped me around the ear.
"I'm the talk of the Wash-House." She continued.
I felt a bit proud.....fancy that, me being the talk of the wash-house...fame at last.

When I eventually came out of School....a red sun was sinking below the smoke belching chimney pots. A rumbling stomach told me that I was starving and wouldn't have gone to the barber's had my life depended on it....which I suppose it did.
My Mother would quite literally murder me.....and what's worse is I'd be sent to bed without any supper...
Jam 'n' Bread and cocoa...the food of dreams.

The thought of School on Monday filled me with dread. It would be "First Bat slap!!" .... "Second Bat Slap!!" .... All day i would be ducking and diving. And at the end of the day, the relief of the last Bat.
My head would be sore and ringing. A new hair cut was always fair game.
I remember Samson and the strength he lost when Delilah cut off his hair and wondered if I should go back to School and attempt to push it down, whilst I still had mine.

Dragging my feet along the way, my thoughts turned to more pleasant things.
I was always hungry....as a result, the thought of tasty grub was never far away. The wonderful aroma from the fish and chip shop had my mouth drooling. It's strange how when you cannot eat something, it seems like you can taste them more.

"Aaaaaahhhhh!!!!" the smell could feed me....but not for long.

It got worse, I had to close my eyes when I passed Noonies Pork Shop window. It's display was a sight for sore eyes...pork, bacon...sausages...and torture for a empty stomach.

Next I passed the Police Station, it brought a smile to my face......When I was a young Bairn, I would enter through the revolving doors and run around in circles....getting nowhere fast. Prompting a Giant Desk Sergeant to wave a big fist at me and threatening to lock me up. High on excitement and dizzy I'd literally fly out of the doors and onto Hedlam Street path..... almost falling flat on my face.

The best part of this mischief was being chased and attempting to run in a straight line on legs that were wobbling through the dizziness. If my Mother ever found out, she would have half killed me....and My Father would have killed the other half.

Pressing my nose against the Pawn Shop window checking that the Chest Expanders were still there, I smiled. The sold label was still on them and with one more payment they would be mine. I left the usual greasy nose print on the shop window glass.

Eventually I finally arrived. The Barbers shop looked like an old sailing ship. Stuck on the pointed corner, bow-windows on each side and above a port holed centre door – dead centre was a huge mast, the red and white barbers pole actually. The Jolly Roger was the only thing missing....mind you, one thing was for sure, Old Hutchy the Barber was anything but Jolly.

You can tell a lot from the look on a man's face, Hutchy's face would scare Vultures from a rotting carcass. He looked like the Devil himself, his long chin wore a seven o'clock shadow and his greasy black hair parted in the centre of a narrow head. He had huge bulbous eye's of an assassin.

His smile looked insane and never left his face.

As a result you never knew what emotions were going on in his head.

A Demon Barber...Old Hutchy wasn't nicknamed Sweeny Todd for nowt!!

His wife Nellie was just the opposite....Fat and Jolly. She ran the pie and peas shop on Raby Street. Her meat pies were famous for they had quite a unique taste. Folk came from far and wide to stand in queues that went half way around the block. The shop was a gold-mine.

Mine You, Lennie Johnston says that he found a lump of gristle that looked similar to an ear-lobe.
However, he wasn't known as Lennie – The – Liar for nothing.
Even so it got you thinking, it didn't take much imagination to see Hutchy as a cut-throat killer....and that brownish/reddish mark on the floor below his chair certainly looked like a blood stain.

A cold shudder ran up my spine as I lifted the little brass door lever...the overhead door bell sprang and sounded its "Ding-a-Ling".
Annoncing my arrival I was sure that someone had walked over my Grave.

An Old man smell of snuff, smoke and stale Beer nearly knocked me on my back. It still wasn't dark outside but it was bleak in here. A naked flame gas mantle hissed and popped as it struggled in vain to bring light for the old men to read yesterdays newspapers. They didn't live in this world, in their's nothing ever changed.

They all looked and dressed the same
Identical to their Fathers and their Grandfathers before them. Flat cap, white silk scarf and their fathers handed down clothes.

They sat silent. Their ghostly pale faces gave them a look of dead men waiting in line for their turn for the next grave.

I couldn't help but wonder if time stood still for them or did they stand still for time. Nobody looked up or took any notice of me.....it was as if I didn't exist, a nobody.....which is exactly what I was.
In those days, in the Company of old men kids were less than nothing.
Maybe it was me who was the ghost, a lost soul....never to rest until he'd had one final hair cut. The ghost that never died.

Maybe if I coughed they might acknowledge me and move along the benches and give this ghost a seat. I did and they didn't. In fact I'm sure the awkward Old Gits shuffled out a bit more. Anyway, even if I did get a seat, it wouldn't be for too long because as soon as the next Old Fella came in I would have to get up and give him my seat. It was an unwritten rule, I couldn't argue with that but it also gave them the right to jump the queue.

Therefore, it wasn't worth taking a seat as I'd be up and down like a yo-yo everytime the door Bell rang.

Only when I was the last in the shop would I become first in the queue... then only for certain when Hutchy turned the OPEN Sign to CLOSED.

So I leaned against the wall and stuck me hands deep into my pockets and spread my legs for balance, anchoring my feet to the floor. Settling for the long wait.

I watched in admiration as Hutchy lathered up and shaved with great skill....lifting the chin, stretching the neck and nose....woooosh.....wooosh – with half a dozen strokes the flashing blade left a wrinkled face as smooth as babies bottom. This didn't last for long, when the master barber removed his grip, the stretched skin and wrinkles rolled back into place.... as quick as the tide coming in. Well oiled polished steel clippers snipped and slid up scrawny necks.

Nothing like the ancient blunt and rusty clippers he used on the Kids... they were more like a lawn mower, nipping, scratching and yanking out great clumps of rooted hair.

The strange thing was when their turn came, the old Fellas hung up their caps....most of them were actually bald.

It was hard not to laugh as Hutchy made such a fuss pretending to cut hair that wasn't there. It was even harder to conceal a smile when he got out a mirror and proceed to show the Men the backs of their head.

"A Grand Job!!" or "Champion Just Champion!!".

They would tell him and he's smile that false smile and take a little bow like an actor on stage. For his swansong he would shake a sprinkling of Brilliantine over a polished head and have the cheek to brush and comb it. One by one the Old Guys would stride out of the Shop, cap pulled down over his ears.

It made me realise that it couldn't be vanity only he knew that he'd had a hair cut and he kept it hidden under his cap.

So it had to be pride. The poor lost souls, nothing in the world but they still had their pride.

Hope if I'm lucky enough to live to their age, I'll still have mine.

There I was standing on a cliff at the edge of the ocean, swaying and tingling with vertigo, when suddenly out of nowhere fingers snapped and a voice boomed..." For Heavens sake boy....Jump to it!!!"

I nearly jumped three feet in the air but it wasn't Gods voice....it was Old Hutchy. I had fallen asleep standing up.

He took one look at my mop of hair.

"Bloody Hell", He moaned... "Will be hear all bloody night."

Talking to the back of my head as I slid down in the chair.

Full of anger he fastened an old worn sheet around my neck, almost strangling me.

Taking a step back he muttered to himself," Could do with some hedge cutters.....Never mind, these Sheep shears will have to do." He Joked.

Standing in front of me now, rubbing his huge hands together and pulling his long boney fingers apart, cracking the joints....he gave me a knowing wink.

I thought to myself," He's getting ready to strangle me!"

Sure enough his strong fingers touched my throat.

I wasn't going to give up on this life without a fight as he moved my neck one way and I pulled it another way.

My life flashed before my eyes....and it wasn't much of a life.

Just as I was about to scream...blue bloody murder, I heard a voice saying," Will you keep your bloody head still you Barmy Sod....I'm trying to cut your hair!!"

Bending my neck into position he began to press and snip as he pushed the old heavy clippers up the back of my neck....Cutting an empty white furrow. Grumbling away to himself whilst puffing away on a cigarette in the corner of his mouth. Fine hairs found their way down the back of my neck....itching and tickling....driving me mad.

The smoke cloud almost choking me.

"Keep your head still....." a Sergeant Majors voice bellowed in my ear, which he had just discovered in a Jungle of Hair. When I looked up and at the mirror, I looked really weird....one ear and half a shaved head.

"Ouch!!!" ....I yelled as he yanked a clump of hair out by the roots
He seemed to snigger as he sheared the clippers over the top of my head. The seat was hard and lumpy, leaving my bottom sore....shuffling from check to cheek to stifle the pain.

"Keep Bloody still!!!" He shouted loudly, this time as he uncovered my other ear. It looked higher up on my head than the other and I breathed a sigh of relief when I remembered that the chair was uneven.

Pushing my head at a different angle he worked away like a professional sheep shearer. Locks of hair cascaded down over my shoulders, floating to the floor. They lay curled up on the floor like dead furry animals.
It was hard not to laugh at the faces I was pulling in the mirror as falling hair tickled my nose.
There was nothing but stubble left on my head when the clipper's finally stopped.
I was cringing at the "Slap – slap – slap – slapping..." sound of the steel sharpening on leather. If I had hair it would have stood on end.
As I got thinking, there was just the two of us in the shop and the doors were locked. I shuddered like an ice cube had been dropped down the back of my neck.
What if the stories I'd heard were true....me, I could end up in the meat pies. I swallowed my Adams apple....and started to whisper my prayers.
Hutchy read my face and he must have read my mind.
He smiled that evil smile looking at his own reflection in the mirror. Then his eyes caught mine and he drew his finger across his throat....Rolling his eyes up into his head.

Me scared....no way, I was bloody terrified. Trembling, I willed myself to be calm. It wasn't easy, not with this voice in my head repeating, "This Lunatic is going to cut your throat."
Hutchy turned his black-dark eyes upwards to heaven and muttered a kind of incantation as he spun the razor on a finger. Like a gunslinger spinning his six shooter revolver.
My neck sank below my shoulders like a tortoise into the safety of its shell.

There was no hiding place, strong fingers gripped tight onto the top of my head like a coconut in a vice.

Yanking it hard, virtually lifting me out of my seat. For a split second I hung there, suspended like a hanged man.

When my neck was suitably stretched he dumped me back down on the seat and jerked my head forward....as though ready for an axe.

"High-ho, High-Ho...its off to work we go..." He sang as the Demon Barber began to scrape my poor head like a turnip.

"Phew." I muttered, sweat was running off my forehead....smarting my eyes.

Gritting my teeth, I winced in pain.

White knuckles gripped the arms of the chair.

We were looking at each other in the mirror, Hutchy like a torturer enjoying his toil and he wasn't going to be happy until I'd been scalped alive.

It was agony, as if a red hot poker was being racked up the back of my neck and over my head.

Something rose in my throat, I didn't know what it was at first.

It was a scream.....which I contained, swallowing I let out a soft whisper...."A..i..eee!!" ....I expected my head to explode as my brain boiled and simmered in my head.

Soft....maybe I was, but I still had my pride and I wasn't going to let him see me cry.

I let out a weary sigh....cursing him under my breath. I pretended to smile and closed my eyes to hold back the tears. Clenching my teeth together as he scraped my now bald head smooth, shiny and red raw.

I died a thousand times...well almost once for sure.

A shower of green foul smelling Brilliantine brought me back to life.

When I opened my eyes, Hutchie was going through the motion of combing hair that wasn't there.

"Okey Dokey...All done and dusted." He joked as he polished the top of my head with a dirty rag.

Then he whipped the sheet off my shoulders like a conjurer revealing his latest trick.....aye, it wasn't hard to imagine Hutchy sawing people in half.

When I looked in the mirror, I thought "Flippin' Heck", I was starring at a funny looking kid with a bald head, flat nose and big ears.....and he was starring at me.

I had laugh and he laughed back.

My legs were stiff and my backside was sore as I heaved myself out of the chair. On legs that were shaking I stood ankle deep in hair.

A heavy hand slapped me on the back, "Ha!!" he laughed wickedly.

"Had yer going there!!" He laughed.

"How'd you mean like?" I replied.

"You should have seen your face.....did I really scare you?" Hutchy asked.

"Nah, not really." I lied forcing a little smile.

"Hadaway to Hell.....I must have done." He pleaded.

"Well....." I admitted," Maybe a little bit."

This seemed to please him as he stated...." Me, I've always wanted to be an actor."

His eyes sparkled as he took a little bow," So, I joined this actors group. Took to it like a brick to water."

"Shouldn't that be a duck to water?" I corrected.

"Whatever." He replied..." Anyway I made a splash....you know I'm only playing the lead role in the next production."

I didn't really want to know but he was waiting for me to ask...so I did,

"What do you call it then....the name, the title of the play?"

He answered "You'll never guess, not in a million years?"

"SWEENEY TODD?" I guessed correctly, Hutchy looked amazed.

"How the Bloody Hell did you know that?" He asked.

"Well to be honest, for a minute there I thought you were going to cut me throat."

His face beamed..." Did you really?"

Hutchy continued...on a roll now," It's all down to practice....mind you I must admit, my Jack The Ripper act does sometimes get carried away."

A maniac glint in his eye...He Conclude," By the way, the month after next we are doing Young Frankenstein.....and if you don't mind me saying so, you'd make a great Lead Role!!"

I had to laugh, I'm not sure if he meant it as a compliment.

"It's our Horror Season.." He added..." And it's awfully hard to find really ugly people these days..."

....or an insult.

"I'll tell you what...." I began..." If your looking for a Wolfman in about six months time....give me a shout!!"
...pointing to myself. "I'm your man."
He looked at me, sounding like an undertaker he said,
"Goodnight young man, and you think about that part."
"I will, I will.." I lied unconvincingly.
"Promise?" He added giving me a knowing wink.
"Cross me Heart." I gave him a nod and a wink back...just to stop myself from saying and hope to die.

The little bell tinkled again as I lifted the door latch, pulling open the door.
I turned and yelled, "I forgot to pay yer?"
Hutchy shook his head..." No son....you hang on to it now for being honest, go and get yourself one of our Steak and Kidney pies for your supper."

"Thanks a lot Mr Hutchinson." I said happily.....
"I'm famished and could eat one pie more than a pig!!"
He laughed and nodded, "I'm sure you could, you're nowt but skin and bone, you need fattening up."
"See ya Mr Hutch...." I called over my shoulder, my hand tight on the sixpence in my pocket.
The bell tinkled again as the Shop door closed.
"Ta-rah!!" I called as I left the shop.

I left the Barbers a new man, shuffling along on unsteady legs...looking like Frankenstein's Monster making his first steps into the world.

Clamming with the hunger...
"Aaaaahhh!!"....I could smell them.
"MMMmmm!!"...I could almost taste them.
Hutchies hot pies...." Nah!!"

"A bag of chips with salt and vinegar please....oh and heaps of tasty, crunching batter scraps." I requested, almost drooling.

I might look daft and Barmy, I can't argue with either....but I am most definitely not stupid.

There wasn't a snowball in Hells chance that I was going to eat one of that bloody Psychopaths meat pies.
Maybe it was all in my imagination but I reckon I came within a whisker of ending up in a Steak an' Kidney Pie.
I believe the only thing that saved me was the fact that there was very little meat on my bones.
Hardly enough to fill a Sausage Roll, never mind a Steak an' Kidney Pie.

Overhead stars twinkled and the moon shone silver on an ink black night sky. I counted my blessings and felt glad to be alive.

I ate my chips and sucked up the crumbs of batter...
"Mmmmmmm...." Smacking my lips.
I drank pure nectar....the wine of the gods....

The vinegar from the corner of the chip bag.

THE END

"Home on the Range"

"Cowboy Dreams...."

"Home on The Range."

It's funny that even now I still laugh when I'm hurt.
But me a hard case?....No, never in the world, it's just the way I am and the way I was brought up.
Mind you, it wasn't really funny at the time.
Well, I can laugh about it now...and I mean really laugh until I cry.

When my memory takes me way back to a time when me and my younger brother were nowt but raggy little matchstick kids in a TS Lowry painted world.
It was a different world then, a world that never changed.
Byker was one square mile of row after row of back to back soot blackened terraced houses. A place of belching chimney stacks, gas lamps, horse drawn carts and cobbled lanes.
Everyone looked the same.
The same as their Mothers and Fathers...and theirs before them.
Most people had nowt.

We had less than nowt, living from hand to mouth.
There's one thing that I did have, something that money couldn't buy.
A wicked sense of humour.
"Wor Marky, your Barmy!!" My Mother often said.
She should know, it was with her and my Fathers help that made me that way. From the day I was born and hopefully until the day I die, I've learned to laugh at life, adversity and mostly at myself.

Maybe that's why even those bad times seem good.
Outside it was bitterly cold and blowing a gale.
Inside wasn't much better, it was draughty and just above freezing.
Me and our kid sat hunched up in front of the cast-iron fire range.
Staring at the fire in the grate.
If we were any closer we'd have been up the flue.
"Wor Marky," Brian my younger Brother asked.
"What would you rather be?" He shivered and placed his hands between his knees.
"What do you mean like?" I answered.
"Cc...Cold or H...Hungry.." His stomach growled....."Or Sss...Scared."
He added and shivered involuntarily.

As if to take the fear of dying away he jokingly continued, "Someone's just walked over my grave!!"

Now that was a tricky question...cold, hungry or scared. It was hard to say.

So I gave a bit of thought to all three.

COLD –

In the grate the fire burned low and I knew for a fact there was no coal left in the coalhouse.

All that remained in there was coal dust and the pungent aroma of cats urine.

The howling gale sounded just like a howling wolf at the door.

I hated the wind, it always seemed to make things worse than what they really were.

The Old House shuddered and creaked against the wind.

Rocked and rolled like an old sailing ship on heavy seas.

The hole in the gas mantle was getting bigger by the minute and roared a blue and orange jet flame through a hole that was more hole than mantle.

Wasting precious gas and only one penny left on the mantle piece to feed the ever greedy gas meter.

HUNGRY –

We were always hungry but never starved.

"There's nowt but skinny mice in our pantry!" We joked at the time.

Once we even found a dead one....we had to laugh, because the joke was on us. The mouse had starved to death, trying to get out.

SCARED –

My Dad....well he put the fear of God into me.

There wasn't a day went by without him threatening to kill us and it was always for nowt!!

To be honest you wouldn't even speak to him let alone catch his eye.

There were no kisses or cuddles in our house....not even a kind word.

"They're all the bloody same to me Wor kid." I replied with ironic laughter in my voice.

We were brought up on all three.

Life was hard and that was a fact of life, you just had to be hard with it.

Me, I ain't complaining, I knew no different, it's just the way it was and always had been. I had learned to expect nothing however, it was harder for him, he was still a Bairn and expected more.

"How do you mean like?" He asked, staring at the fire's glowing embers, mesmerised.

I looked down at him saying, "Oh like I said they're all the same to me. If it's not one then it's one of the others."

He looked up from the fire and asked, "Well what happens if you're in all three at the same time!!"

I didn't have the heart to answer that....I stayed silent.

With that he continued..."Well me Wor Marky....I think it's a lot worse to be in all of them at once."

He spat into the coal embers looking sorry for himself.

I did feel sorry for him but I would'nt show it..." Don't be soft, there's a lot worse off than us. One day we'll look back and laugh and call these the good old days."

"Aye!" He moaned...." That'll be the day."

He watched his spit sizzle and hiss on the red coal.

With a sigh he stated, "Wish I had a dog?"

"So do I..." I Joked..."I'd bloody well eat it!!"

Our Brian was always wishing his life away.

While he wished for the moon...Me, I'd be happy just looking at the stars.

Our mother came out of the dark kitchen, bow-legged, biceps bulging with the weight of a huge soot-blackened, cast iron pan.

"Get away back from the fire!!" She shouted..."Let the dog see the rabbit."

"Whoopee!!" Our Kid yelled at the very thought of food – as only the hungry can.

"Rabbit Pie!!!" He guessed....

..."I love rabbit pie me, especially the crust." He was beaming.

That was short lived as me Mam replied, "The only crust you'll be getting my bonny Lad is the crust off the old Loaf, because there isn't any flour left. So we'll just call this rabbit stew."

She plonked the heavy pan onto the hob.

"Now..." She said loud and clear...

..."It's been on a low-light on the gas stove for a while, so it's just about half cooked."

She nodded her head in the direction of the pan, "And I want you two to keep an eye on it...you both got that!!"

We nodded our heads in tandem and both said, "Aye Ma!!"

She went on...." An' mind you stir the pan now and again."

She demonstrated a stirring movement, smiling," So as it don't burn it's arse out!!"

"Now don't you two forget.....or else!!" She threatened, waving a fist in the air.

Actions speak louder than words I thought.

As she left the room she shouted back, "I'm off across the Back Lane to Minnie Headley's for a bit of chat and hopefully borrow a pail of coal..... you two had better behave!!"

"Ma....when will it be ready?" Brian shouted back.

"When it's done and not before." She said sarcastically.

"Aaaww....but I'm starving." He pleaded, holding his belly.

She leaned close to him and said quietly, "And Brian my son, are you ever anything else?", she smiled and gave him a clout around the ear.

"Ouch....what's that for?" He cried looking cross eyed.

Mam gave a little righteous nod before answering," That my bonnie lad is before you start."

I had to laugh because there was no arguing with that.

The both of them were always giving us a clip for nowt.

You could say they were pretty generous when it came to handing out clouts around the head.

At this moment I instinctively ducked my head down and sure enough a heavy right hand went sailing over my head.

"Greedy eyed sods." She said with a weary sigh.

As she went bounding down the back stairs, muttering to herself, "You would think I never fed them.....their eye's are bigger than their bellies."

The latch clicked as she opened the back door, she yelled her final instructions up the stairs as if she was the Captain leaving the ship, "There's a penny on the mantle piece for the gas meter and don't you dare poke that fire." she warned, "....or I'll bloody well murder you!!".

The back door slammed shut.

Staring at the pot on the fire, Wor Brian said longingly, "I thought we were having rabbit pie?" He moaned...."I Love rabbit pie me."

"Think of it as rabbit pie without the crust." I told him, "...and you know what, you couldn't have made a pie with that rabbit anyway."

"How's that then?" He asked curiously.

"Simple man...." I gave him a knowing wink. "You need a hump- backed rabbit for a pie."

"What for like?" He replied giving me a puzzled look.

"Think about it!"....and I nudged him in the arm..."You need the hump to keep the crust up!!"

He turned and looked up at me in wonderment...he opened his mouth to speak, but only a weary sigh came out.

Time dragged by as it does when you are hungry and waiting to be fed.

The last Penny was put into the Gas Meter.

The light brightened.....not by very much.

However, it was bright enough to give Brian the bright idea of making shadows on the wall.

Clenching his fist and putting up two fingers he made a large shadow of a rabbit on the cracked-distempered stained wall.

"Look Wor Marky....a rabbit!!!" He yelled.

Flattening my hand and bending my index finger I stuck up my thumb.

"Look a Greyhound!" I said...."And, it's eating your rabbit!!"

"Just imagine...." Wor young 'un said dreamy-eyed, "If you could be anyone in the world....who would you be?"

It was his favourite game....always dreaming of being somebody else.

I used to tell him when he grew up he would...we all would.

But the trick is never forget where you came from and who you were.

I told him what he wanted to hear, just as I had told him many times before.

"Me!!...." I said pointing to myself, "I'd want to be a Cowboy....riding on the range."

"Me too....partner!!" His face lit up as his imagination galloped away.

"You and me, we'd ride the range together." He smiled.

"We certainly will....you bet your goddam life we will."...I drawled in my best John Wayne impression.

"Yes....we'd live on bacon and beans..." He almost sang.

"And sleep under the stars..." He revisited his dream.

Looking at me for reassurance he continued...." And sing cowboy songs... don't forget the cowboy songs."

He looked at me almost pleading, as if I agreed, it would happen.

"Aye..." I said, "We'll sing our lungs out....every starry night, snug and warm around the blazing camp fire. By the light of the silvery moon, singing them Cows to sleep."

"Great!!" he yelled... "...But we'll have our suppers first...."

Nodding his head and rubbing his belly, he stated, "You can't sing cowboy song's on an empty stomach."

"Definitely..." I agreed, "We'll be so full of bacon and beans...we'd fart along to the tunes."

He really laughed at that and started to sing. "Home...home on the range.."

Putting our heads together we harmonized, "Where the deer and the antelope play..." And just for the fun of it we tried to fart in tune.

"Where seldom is heard a discouraging word...."

But between the two of us.... "Where the clouds are not cloudy all day..." ....there wasn't a decent fart to be had.

So we yodelled at the end of the song..." Yippee....kye...oh...kye... aaaayy!!!"

The back door slammed shut with a bang, bringing us back home from the range and a yell up the stairs, "I'm back....", brought us back to reality.

Mam came in with a draught of cold night air.

"Couldn't borrow a pail of coal." She said, "So I ended up with this one great big lump!"

She clutched it under her arm wrapped in news paper.

Unwrapping the lump of coal, she rolled in onto the hearth.

Straightening the paper, she read from the front page.."Pah, bloody News of The World.." She crumbled up the paper into a ball.

"It's a dirty rotten paper..." She muttered..."Don't you two ever dare read it mind, all its good for is lighting the fire and wiping your backside.

With that she threw it onto the fire. "Good riddance." She stated as it burst into flames.

I didn't have clue what she was on about, neither of us could hardly read.

Oor Wullie and the Broons was just about our level.

Even so, I made a mental note in my head – breaking up the coal with the poker – Just as soon as I could read....I would start reading the News Of The World.

"MMmmmm...." Mam said as she tasted the stew with a wooden spoon.
"That'll put meat on your bones." She finished.
"You two should eat slower...you've got no manners at all." Mam called.
Her advice fell on deaf ears.
Mouths wide open, level with the bowl....we spooned it in rapidly.
"Are you two listening to me....you're like a couple of pigs."
We both grunted that we had heard.
"Please Ma..." Wor young 'un begged in his best Oliver Twist voice,
"Can I have some more?" ...it made me laugh.
He was wasting his time.
"No....your both greedy little swine's!!" Mam scolded.
"....Your eye's are bigger than your Bellies!"
She was right about that.
Given the chance, I would eat one tatty more than a pig.
"Let's pull the wish bone?" Brian suggested.
He held a twisted bone in a bent little finger and I had to laugh when he closed his eyes as the bone snapped.
I never had the heart to tell him rabbits don't have wish bones....Do they?

....

In the local boozer, what a grand fella he was.
The life and soul of the party...generous to a fault.
A smile never left his face.
On Leaving the Bar, it was pats on the back....shaking of hands, "Good old Willy..." Everybody's best mate.
The moment he stepped into the real world, a remarkable change came over him like a werewolf in a full moon....only he did not need the moon.
A real life Dr Jeckyll and Mr Hyde...that was me Dad.
As he marches along Gas Lit cobbled streets'...
..A roll of thunder in the distance heralds his coming.
The thunder clapped louder this time....We both shuddered.
"It's the Devil with his clogs on." Brian recited.

"Nah Son..." Me Mother smiling..."It's that drunken Old Sod...in his work boots, on his way home.

The villain of the peace came clattering up the bare wood creaking stairs.
Cursing and swearing as he came.
"Daddie's Home!" Mam joked.
Snarling and growling he burst through the door.
"Where's me bloody dinner woman!!" He demanded.
"Out of my bloody way..." He Growled and took his usual swing at us.
I ducked out of the way, our Young 'un yelled ..."Ouch!!"
He was still far too slow. One day he would learn to read dads face.
It wasn't easy...He'd just as soon give you a clip over the ear for nowt with a smile on his face as well as a snarl.

Dad sat hunched up, dead centre of the fire with a huge bowl...heaped full with steaming hot stew on his lap.
A smug look on his face...starving with a drunken hunger...he was really looking forward to his meal.
Too hot to eat, he blew on a spoon heaped with stew.
Out of the side of his mouth he snarled..." I bet you two greedy eyed sods would love to eat this lot?"
In the scullery Mam looked out of the small window while we were having our bed time wash under the cold water tap in the sink.
"Bloody begrudged..." He shouted louder this time as he blew on the spoon of hot stew.
"Take no notice lads." Said Mam as we rubbed ourselves dry with the end of a raggy towel each....And I wished to God!!!
"Take the bloody bread out of a workin' mans mouth!!!" He Bellowed with anger.
Then it happened...it wasn't what I had wished for but it came pretty close.
Just as he lifted the spoon towards a wide open mouth...
A brilliant flash of lightning lit the room...
BOOOMMMM!!!!!....The thunder clap that followed shook the house.
As we came through the door an avalanche of soot came hurtling down the chimney flue.....gushing out of the fireplace, smothering Dad.
Call it instinct, call it reflex, call it whatever you like...
Anyway, Dad moved pretty quickly for a drunken old man sitting in a

haunch. He didn't just jump...he exploded!!

A bald head came out of a cloud of soot & smoke, like a rocket out of a bottle.
At the same time Dad's head smashed against the gas mantle and drew blood.
The bowl of stew splattered the walls and ceiling with a loud squelch!!
On his descent...he yelled a delayed, "Ooouuchh!!!" or it might have been an, "Ooowww!!"......but it was definitely an "Ooommphh!!" as his boney backside landed back on the couch, sending the creaking springs right down to the floor.

Now it's a well known fact that springs are not called springs for nothing and in this case, they lived up to their name...springing back with a vengeance, launching Dad from whence he came.
Out of a cloud of smoke, a soot blackened bald head shot up like a cannon ball from a gun.
Alas, halfway up, his head met the Bowl of stew on its way down.
Well it's a known fact that a falling object gains weight with every foot it falls.
That coupled with the speed of Dad's upward thrust on take off.
When the Bald head and bowl made contact, it sounded like an egg shell being hit with a spoon....There was one hell of a crack.
Dad came down to earth like a shot bird...bouncing off the couch...landing onto the mat...out to the world.
His face covered in blood, soot and stew...he looked like the monster from the black lagoon.
"Is he dead?" Wor young 'un asked...more in hope than concern.
"Nah!!" Mam answered.."He's only dead drunk...The Devil looks after his own."

Mam reflected, "Phew....what an awful night!" She had a good right to complain..."It never rains, it pours!!"
"Don't you worry Mam...." I tried to console her.
"Look at the bright side...things cannot get any worse?" I said
"Well can they?" I queried.
And sure enough, just to prove me wrong, Zoooom!!!!
A flash of sheet lightning...it's glare lit the room ghostly white before

blinding us.

The thunder clap that followed a split second later deafened us and we were all struck dumb when the Devil did a hell of a clog dance.

There was a swishing noise and a putt...putt...putting sound.....the gas went out!!

....

Oh yes....I can laugh about it now and I mean really laugh until I cry.

But me a hard case...nah, never in the world.

You see, sentimental songs bring a tear to my eye and just the very thought of kids suffering just about breaks my heart. Me, I'm as soft as clart's.

Unless someone tries to steal the food out of my mouth or tries to scare me then I'm warning you....look out!

I'm a bit of a villain when roused, can't help it.

It's just the way I am...the way I was dragged up.

THE END

**"Da' didn't just jump he
exploded!!"**

END OF

PART ONE

The Byker Lion

▣ *PART TWO*

The Last Navvy

The Last Navvy

(A Hard Day's Graft)

By Mark James

"HARD DAY'S GRAFT."

■ I left school hardly able to read or write, and hid the fact by going into a life of hard graft.. Even so, I loved the bloody work in my younger days, the harder the better. Well, I had a chip on my shoulders and felt I had to prove myself. I've laid bricks, stone, concrete and tarmac, all on bonus...but the hardest by far, was the some eighteen years I spent as a Navvy, digging mile after mile of track. We laid the cables underground and were paid by the yard.

Really hard work is like a drug, once it gets hold of you, it ends up taking over your whole life. The harder the work, the harder a man becomes.
You haven't time for your family and kids. It's just work, sleep, work, sleep.....Oh aye...and the booze an' all.
Without the drink there'd be no sleep, even with a belly full of beer, it was still hard to stop the mind from working the night-shift.

"Pet....pet..the alarm's gone off, you're going to be late for work."
"By Christ, I'm knackered....what day is it love?"
"E-er...Saturday...no, Sunday....no it's Monday, definitely Monday."
"Monday, nivva in the world...where the hell did the bloody weekend gan?"

....

Outside *The Bay Horse*, the men stand hunched up, hands deep in pockets, heads bowed, propped against walls, lamp-posts and shop doors. Unshaven, bad with the beer and full of hell. The fag they drag on gives little comfort. Better watch what your saying on a Monday mornin', the start of another back breaking week.

Even though I'm sick of me life, I put on a face an' joke.
"It's a great day for graft lad's!!!" I'm greeted with a barrage of curses.

"Hello Jack, how's it gannin'?" I ask.
"Oh fine, just fine...an' how's yu'self?"
"Me!! A'm just as fit as a bloody lop." I lie..."A'm rarin' to go."

Big Jack Casey...he's a great fella is Jack. A Farm lad, more at home walking over ploughed fields, with that high stepping stride of his.

He left seven brothers an' five sisters, him being the eldest, to make his fortune. Land is cheap in Donegal, the farms are small. He'll be the proud owner, on his return...and that won't be long now he promises himself, two years or thereabouts. And won't he still be a fine young fella, never did know his date of birth, so he'll forever stay in his prime.

Aye, *"Roll on.."*, he keeps reminding himself, but until then he'll dream his dreams, of green land an' the lovely Colleens, with a permanent smile and eyes that only ever stay half open.

Bone-broken nose, he'll fight any man. A bull of a fella is **John O'Grady**.

"How's it gannin, John lad?"

John's a man of few words, nods his reply with a dreamy eyed smile and goes back again to his Galloway Bay, the Sea and the small fishing boat... he himself will own. O'aye, a fisherman, that's all he ever wanted to be... and what a catch he'll make for the local girls, by Christ!!...he could take his pick.

"One of these days"...as he takes a deep breath, he can almost smell and hear the Sea.

Naw!! It's just that dirty owld bugga Patsy pissing against the wall.

"Hello there, Mick lad, how's it gannin'?"

Might as well talk to me arse, too much on his mind has Mick in the mornin'.

Black Mick, as bright as a dark night and as strong as a horse.

Mick lives his entire life half-way between day-dream and nightmare.

He married a muscular tattooed local slag, with the face that would frighten vultures off a dead donkey. With the drink in him, he saw her as a rare beauty,..huh!!...he's stayed drunk ever since. Now there's six little black Micks, an' one on the way. He'll never be able to go back to his beloved home land to face the locals and the childhood sweet-heart he left behind with a kiss and a promise...he'd be back to wed her just as soon as he'd made his fortune.

Funny.....he never told lies then, but then again neither did he smoke, drink, gamble nor bloody swear.

Patsy O'Brian the owld fella of the gang. The drummer up...fryer of meals...the brewer of tea...filler of safety lamps. He'd rather be kicking out with the boys...too true, so he says. The owld fraud.

"G'd mornin' pat."

"Piss off!!"

Ha! Aye that's Pat alright, miserable owld sod. He was bloody well born awkward that one.

Terry Malloy, a rough hewn mountain of a man, reads the newspaper as he ambles on his way to graft. He's in no hurry, he's fallen in love with the big buxom girl on page three.

Terry should by rights be wearing glasses and a hearing aid, but he's too proud. He should go an' see about his feet an' back, but can't be bothered. Worst of all, are the piles that hang from his arse like a bunch of grapes. He's the top ganger man an' proud of it......an' hard as nails. He'll drop to bits, or die just trying to prove it!

Little Billy Craggs lives in the posh end of Gosforth, where he plays his golf, because, that's what the posh people do.....and he tries to talk, *"like wot they do"*. He's bossed by a spoilt brat of a daughter, hen-pecked by a snob of a wife and pissed on by her miniature French poodle. But when it comes to work he's a far different man, Little Billy is a big man. Smoking a big cigar an' dressed to kill, he pulls up in a big flash car, paid for by us, robbed from our bonus. Like most gaffers, he's never done a hard days work in his life, but loves to talk about it. He looks down on the men with contempt.

"Bloody animals, all of them, all they live for is boozin', gamblin', fightin' and women. They sub every day, come pay-day, they've nowt to lift. Worn out with the graft, old men before their time and not knowing when the cap would be passed for them, to pay for an early wake. Hell-raisers they may be today, but come tomorrow, I'll see them in bloody hell!!"

A right pain in the arse is little Billy Craggs. The men laugh at him and call him, *"little shit house"* behind his narrow back.

....

Pat Lacey thunders over the Tyne Bridge, cursing the traffic, the weather and their Lass for not setting the alarm clock.

The wagon gears grind in protest as he struggles to change them. He tells a honking motorist the impossible, *"Go an' stuff yu'sel'!!"* and gives him a two fingered salute. Jumping the red light he jerks forward, turns the corner on two wheels and heads towards the Bay Horse in a cloud of diesel smoke. God help anyone who gets in his way.

A convoy of waiting wagons stand revving-up. Gruntin' an' groaning we climb over the tail-board to be swallowed up by the tied down shack. The pong of sweaty owld clothes, baccy and stale beer are awful hard to digest.

- ◼ On my left foot I tie my foot iron, it's worth its weight in gold. We work alone, some 12 yards apart, facing one another's backs. In less than an hour, my shirt will be wringing with sweat and I'll be stripped down to the waist.

- ◼ To make top bonus, a drum length of 500 yards, 2 ft 6" deep. Just over a shovel width, has to be dug the same day, ready for the long pull in the morning. So it's flat out from the word go. The top soil is cast to one side, the clay on the other, this makes it easier to back-fill.

....

The starting is the hardest, the first hour is always the worst. The smell hangs in the air, the stink of sweat and men breaking wind, after the drinking bout of the night before. It takes will power to get the body started. I curse myself, grit my teeth and get mad at the hard bone-jarring ground....and the world...but mostly myself for only being human. Hissing and snarling, I set about my task. *"It'll get easier."*, I tell myself and hope and pray to God for my second wind.

A wonderful feeling grows as I get into my stride. The tools feel light in my hands....the energy flows. With the sun on my back, bursting with power, on days like these I could take on the bloody world.

Sweat rolls off me, the salt stinging my eyes, by Christ, I could do with a nice cool drink.........roll on the night, an' a couple of pints.

Even though I work in the most beautiful countryside, I'm blind to the beauty, I only see a hard day's graft in front of my eyes.
Steel strikes steel, as foot iron boot drives hard down on the spit, pile-driving the long narrow blade into the hard ground.
The clay is sliced into long narrow blocks and heaved up and over my left shoulder, with a flick of the wrist it leaves the silver blade.
Two draws of the grafting-tool, then crumb up with the shovel, that's the depth, the tape measure is in my head....Then it's onto the next stretch.

Aye, it's a race, there's no denying that...maybe's a race to an early grave. The change over to top gear is automatic, my only purpose in life is to tear out the ground. Blood flows into pumped-up, rock hard muscles.... through cord-like veins. This power you'll savour in old age, but bugger old age, I feel immortal on days like today.
It's only now that I can laugh at the un-wisdom of it all....but in my prime, I felt great to be setting the pace.
The clock in my head with the help of hunger pangs in my stomach, tell me it's nearly time for breakfast. Eleven o'clock, owld Patsy makes a start on the fry-up. It's the smell that hits you first.....right in the pit of an empty stomach, bringing on the starvation.

Can still smell it . . . .

'GRUB UP'

Can still taste it. . . . . .

"Grub up lads......lets be havin' yu's!!" The yell of Patsy's gravel voice is like an angels' song to my ears.

As one, the gang downs tools and scrambles from the trench, it's the first time we've straightened our backs, by Christ it's hard to stand up-right.

All eyes look backwards to admire, over the greenest of fields, 300 yards of track which lies straight as a die.

Hands on hips, we stretch, then swagger away, trying to hide the agony of a broken back.

....

A fire-devil stands outside the canvas shack. A frying pan as big as a bin lid sizzles on the glowing coke.

Its contents are mouth watering: -- Steak, onions, sausages, eggs and black pudding.

Patsy O'Brien, the drummer up, stands grinning rightly proud. It's no easy task to cook outside in all weathers for a bunch of starving navvies that could eat a scabby horse!

The grub is dished out and eaten with bare hands. In an orgy of gluttony... riving an' tearing at the meat. Cleaning plates with doorstep slices of bread, covered by half an inch of thick butter.

Washing it down with strong, sweet, scalding hot tea, out of an enamel bucket full to the brim. The tea looked and tasted like treacle...the tin pots went in time after time, as we made up for lost sweat.

The men, all Irish, were the grandest bunch of scoundrels I've ever known... and the best grafters. This was definitely the finest gang I'd ever worked with. You've got to work and drink with men before you really know them, and prove you are as good...if not better at what you are about. It's a great feeling, I felt like a King....if only in a small kingdom.

Tea break over, I could gladly go to sleep for a week, but it's back to graft.

Time flies when you're happy at your work. Towards afternoon, that's the time of day when everything seems right with the world, anything seems possible. The feeling is as close to heaven as I have ever been. Even so, i know for a fact, that before this day's shift is over....i'll feel nearer to bloody hell.

Late afternoon...the mind starts to wander, it's the first sign of fatigue that. I daydream of daft things that happened a long time ago....places I used to visit as a bairn...forgotten faces. I try to figure out where I went wrong, but my mind is like a book with no reading and the pictures tell lies.
Could I really have changed anything? ....could I bloody hell!!

Sweat rolls off me and mixes with the muck and grime, on a body that now starts to ache all over, but still I must ignore the strain......my pace mustn't slacken.

Come four o'clock, owld Patsy brings a bucket of good strong tea. It's drunk sitting at the side of the track. Ten minutes' rest, a bit of crack, then off we go on the last lap. The tea renews lost energy. I'll stay ahead...it's only daft pride, I'll not let up, nor will they. The rivalry is friendly but it's always there. Nearly time to knock off, I'm about buggered but I musn't show it.
I keep these feelings to myself. The tools become heavy and awkward in my hands, the strength drains from a body that no longer belongs to me. I work in slow motion...sick in the guts, I'm going through hell, ready to drop, and I wish to Christ the ganger would blow the bloody whistle!

It's gone six o'clock....there's a hammerin' deep in my skull that leaves me dizzy and light headed....I'm nearly at deaths door, for God's sake you long streak of shit, blow that bloody whistle.
I grin at the rotten sod through clenched teeth...never show the bugger your beat!!.... The shrill blast is sweet music to my ears.

The shack is hoisted on to the high-backed wagon and roped down for the second time in the day, we crawl over the tail board, more dead than alive...with a shudder then a jerk, away we go....50 miles to home.
That bloody driver hits every bump on the road!!

Bones weary and stiff as owld Nick, I sit, slumped over, my arms are numb, they hang wearily by my sides, my head is heavy, eyelids fight to keep away the sleep. Half-dreamt dreams drift wearily through my mind, but my aching limbs keep me awake and for the first time today I look at the sky.

There's a great atmosphere as the blarney starts to flow, making up for

166

the long silence of the day. It's called blaggarding and always ends up in a good laugh. We call each other worse than shite, it's hard to keep a straight face.

Seven o'clock at night, the wagon pulls up outside the Central Station. By Christ!! What a sight we must look, un-shaven, black faces and clarty boots, like a wagon load of tramps. The men jump over the back like bundles of old rags, nearly breaking their necks and cursing the driver for pulling away too soon.

With a proud swagger, we roll into the pub across the road. The first pint doesn't touch the sides. The big talk starts, former work-mates join in the bragging and the winking of eyes' as the boys try to out do each other, it's all great crack.

The beer is swilled down, numbing body and brain, making a man twice the man he ever was...he'll be a half dead man, come the morn'. But tonight I feel like superman, but in truth I can hardly stand, never mind bloody fly. Closing time, shaking hands, pats on the back, I'm everyones' best pal. Come tomorrow we'll be sober and callin' each other worse than shite again...bloody well great life innit!!
I feel immortal, well, more like mortal drunk anyway.

....

The sound of a bell miles away, brings me back from the dead. A tired female voice is saying, *"Pet...pet, the alarm's gone of, you'll be late for work.. yu will...yu will!!"*

The rhythm of the alarm clock repeats over and over, that it's the time to get up.

I could sleep forever....But!!

........................It's the start of another day!!

THE END

Back breaking...................................

Bonus making..............

"O' Rileys' Run."

Instinctively, we gripped the edge of the hard bench...our arses went bumpity...bumpitty...bumpitty...bump!!
As the bloody driver hit every bump in the narrow winding road.
We all cursed as the wagon jerked and ground to a halt.

I was one of the gang of Navvies, in the days when most digging was done by hand.
This job, a 5 mile cable run on a beautiful stretch of the Northumberland Coast.
The high tension cable had to be 2ft 6inches deep.
We were on bonus...paid by the yard.
A drum length was 250 Yards, to make top bonus, the five of us...'Riley, Don, Arkie, Black Mick and Myself...the one and only Geordie in the gang.
We had to dig out the trench, pull the cable, back fill and shift the surplus all in the same day. It was hard graft, there was no denying that, but they were a great bunch of lads...we always had a good laugh.
Come rain, snow or blow.....nowt stopped us...well nearly nowt.

....

The bull, a large Aberdeen Angus, stood fetlock deep in water, his breath writhed around his nostrils.....he guarded his domain.

The grass and the wild flowers were laden with dew, which sparkled in the early morning sunshine.
I turned to O'Riley, who was always full of hell in the mornin'.
"Great day for graft O'Riley..."
"Piss off yu eejit...me feet's soaken an' am bad with me guts."...O'Riley moaned.
I stripped to the waist, strapped my foot-iron on and began to dig.
"Aaaaah." I took me a deep breath, taking it all in.
"Will yer smell that fresh-air Mick Lad......bloody well great man!!"
Black Mick had just started to dig, slow...and painfully.

"Bloody hay-fever!" he moaned and stopped to blow his nose on a dirty hanky.

Bees were buzzing above the giant thistles. Thank God the midgies' and most of the flies' had gone.
I yelled over my shoulder...."Arkie!!"
"Aye?"
"Where do the flies gan in the winter?"
"Fly-land." Joked Arkie, not bothering to look up from his task.

"Git that fresh air down yer lungs." I yelled down the line to Don.

Don was digging with a fag glued to his lower lip. He coughed half his guts up before answering. Looking up he took in the view.
"No bettin' shop......no boozer.....worra bloody wilderness." He moaned.
"Wake up man." I joked... *"Git Yer head outa' yer arse...an' smell the roses."*
Don grinned, but tried to hide it by twisting up his craggy face.
"Will yer hush, yer big draft Geordie lunatic." Said he driving down hard on the spit.

The diggin' was soft, we tore out the ground.....

The cattle were lazing in the shade under the trees, and the birds were singing their lungs out. The sun was high, we'd made great progress....... must be nearly 150 Yards across the field, another 100 and we'd have a drum length.

The Angus Bull lay in the dip, a natural hollow where a cool stream ran through. It's giant head swivelled like a tank turret, red furnace eyes scanned the horizon.
The moment the men had entered the field, the bull had declared.. **"WAR"**!!

....

Arkie scrambled out of the trench he'd just finished. He stood on the heap of freshly dug muck.
"Is that a bull over there!!" he said to himself, shielding his eyes from the sun.

The Bull had become crafty. When young, he'd charge at the drop of a hat....or in his case...a red-rag.

Not anymore!!...over the years, he'd learnt self discipline. Cool & calm... was now the name of the game.

Patiently, he'd waited for the men to work their way nearer to the centre of the field...the point of no return, then and only then....he'd make his move.

"It's a bloody cow." I joked.

"And anyway, so what!!...if it's a bull...it's gotta be harmless."

"And how's that like?" O' Riley argued back...and went on to say something about a crafty bull he once knew.

"I think," ...I went on to remind the lads..."*If it was dangerous, it would have made it's move by now....well wouldn't he!!"*

They all nodded their heads in agreement, muttered something, and went back to graft...

The predator lay in wait, weighing up the situation and letting the men get a false sense of security. All the time looking for the weakest in the man-pack...the slowest...the dumbest!!

O' Riley farted..."*Am away for a shit..*" Said he, ambling towards a clump of bushes. Going down on his haunches, O'Rileys' curly grey head disappeared from view...

That's when he made his move...

"Sure that's a bull." Says Arkie.

The heat of the sun dried out the land, the mist coiled and curled around the giant Oak trees.

The Angus bull sneaked up in the mist. He'd a wicked glint in his fire-devil eyes.

O' Riley was busy wiping his arse and singing...

"If you ever go across the sea to Ireland."

When he got to, *"Maybe at the closing of your day."*.....
"Yee-eeee-k!!!!" He let out a blood curdling scream.

When I looks up, there was owld O'Riley.....coming out of the bushes like a greyhound out of the traps. I reckon he was moving pretty fast considering...Considering he was pulling up his pants and struggling to get his braces over his shoulders.
"Will yer look at him go." Says Black Mick.
"Wouldn't yer think he'd be too owld to be racing that Bull at his age."
"A fiver on der Bull!!" Says Arkie.
"Tis' a fine lookin' Bull." Says Don
"Will yer look at him go...now yer wouldn't think he'd have it in him, now would yer!!" Says Mick.

O'Riley, head down, arse up, bound on his bandy legs over the rough terrain. Down the sloping field he ran towards the nearest hedge-row.

"A fiver on the Owld fella!!" Says Don, spitting on the palm of his open hand.................Arkie took him up on the bet, they shook hands on it.

O'Riley ran like the Devil himself was after him.....and maybe he was. Demented, the Bull thundered after him, as un-stoppable as a locomotive.

I'm ashamed to say, I bet on the Bull.

O'Riley was doing great, until....a cow pat as big as a bin-lid lay in his path.
It's skin baked and set like a pie crust by the Sun.
O'Riley's running foot came down hard. The cow pat burst and erupted like a Volcano....he skated on green slime. Whirling forward, arms spinning as he tried to stay upright, like a surfer on a wave.....of cow-shit!!

Ejecting from the dung, O'Riley did a somersault, with half a twist...We gave him 9 out of 10 for style...but changed it for a 5, when he landed on his head, bouncing as high as himself in height.
I think that confused the Bull....for a split second, he broke his stride.

We looked on in wonder, as O'Riley did the impossible and landed on his feet without so much as breaking his stride.....Flabbergasted, we had to give him 10 out of 10 for recovery, when he hit the ground running.

The Bull was gaining fast and breathing down his neck.
"I'll wager He'll make it over the gate." Said Don.
No one took the bet. There was a chorus of *"Ooh's"* and *"Aaah's"* from us as O'Riley ran fast, un-hesitant paces...approaching the gate like an Olympic high-jumper, with a hop, skip and a.....alas, he never got the chance to jump. On the skip, just as He was about to launch himself over the top rail, the Bull's battering ram of a head, caught him on the hop.
O' Riley, being bow-legged, he took the brunt of the murderous blow in the goolies............ "**ooooyahh!!!!**" He wailed like a siren.

As if propelled by explosives he rocketed through the air.
Have you ever seen a human cannon-ball,....Well, that was O'Riley.

O'Riley lay unconscious for half an hour.
Don splashed two bucket fulls of water over him.
Arkie massaged his knee-caps.
Mick went for an ambulance.
Me............i fanned his goolies with my shirt.

Like a Red-Indian on the trail of the foe, Mick tip-toed through the grass verge towards the hole in the hawthorn hedge. In his right hand, a pick shaft, he held it like a war-club. The Angus bull stood grazing, his rump faced the gap in the hedge. His testicles were enormous, they hung like a couple of punch-balls, dangling in the grass.

Down on one knee, one eye closed, Mick sighted the bulls testicles along the length of the pick-shaft, like a snooker player about to pot the black... Mick's eyes measured the distance.
Turning his head he looked over his shoulder, to where we his audience stood on the back of the wagon....wide eyed and gob-smacked.
Mick had a wicked glint in his eye and he winked before changing his grip on the shaft.
He now held it like a battering-ram. Slowly and methodically he swung the shaft....to and fro. We all held our breath!!
Once....twice, it gained momentum. On the third swing the pick-shaft

came down in a blur and shot forward with all Micks might.......the wide end of the pick-shaft hit the bull-balls dead centre.

Mick yelled *"Git-up yer bugga!!.....*on impact the bulls-balls shot sideways. One in each pocket.

Next morning, the Angus Bulls' red furnace eyes scanned the horizon.

Fear and fury filled him mad with rage.

On the moment the men entered the field, he charged with every pound of force.

It came sooner than I expected, we'd only just closed the gate.

There was an explosion of hooves as the Bull thundered towards us.

"Thought you says it wouldn't bother us anymore. Doctor-bloody-Doolittle." I yelled at Black Mick.

"Just wait Geordie lad,..just wait. Stand yer ground."

"Yer must be jokin'." Says Arkie....getting back over the gate.

Don was right behind him.

Me....i'm a bit of a coward, just call it whatever you like, Geordie pride or just plain daft.......Anyway, I stayed with Mad Mick.

Closer and closer it come, like a giant black-bat out'a Hell!!..bearing down on us.

"Look him in the eyes." Said Mick.

That was easier said than done.

The blue-black nose of the beast pointed at me...like a double barrelled shotgun.

Riveted to the spot...........i said my prayers.

My life flashed before my eyes, it didn't take long.......didn't have much of a life. And just when it was about to end, Mick yelled through cupped hands at the top of his voice, *"Git-up-yer-Bugga!!"*

In a flash, the Bulls' testicles sent an S.O.S. to it's brain.

He stopped dead in his tracks, as if hit by a bazooka.

He took off on earth shaking, thundering hooves...screaming like a banshee, as he went back to where he'd came from.

Me and Mick watched him disappear from view...'til he became only a tiny black dot on the horizon.

"*Scared...........me....Naw!!*" I lied to the lads.
Then I told the truth......."*I think I've just pissed me pants...*"
Mick turned and said with a sickly grin, "*Think yersel lucky.............i've just shit mine.*"

We went up to see O'Riley at the hospital.
The swelling's gone down....he's up and about. I couldn't help but laugh... he walks like a ruptured duck.

Reckon he'll be out soon.

Gave me a dirty look when he opened the brown paper bag I'd fetched him. Thought I'd surprise him, with the biggest pair of plums I'd ever laid eyes on. O'Riley stared at them with wounded pride.

"*Yer dirty rotten Bastard!!*" He uttered. With a smile that might have easily been mistaken for a look of pain.
O'Riley held the big bluey-black plums...

One in each hand......................

THE END

Just a thought..........................

'O'Rileys Run'

"MURPHY'S MIRACLE."

Me, I'm bloody well knackered, fightin' to keep me eyes open, half dreamt dreams come and go as I gaze outa' the back of an open waggon. Might be here in body, but me spirit is still in a nice warm bed snuggled up to Wor Lass.

The wagon thunders on it's way, straight as a die along the old Roman Military Road.

Me and the Boys, a bunch of lunatic Navvies are on our way to graft... We are Contracted to lay electric cables under ground, on bonus, paid by the yard...

- ▣ The job can be easy or hard, depending on the elements and how hard the ground is.
  All we have to do is dig out a trench 3ft deep – Jack up the drum – pull the cable & back fill.
  Then do it again & again, mile after mile.
  Whey aye man, it's as simple as that.....like I say's, the job's a doddle.
  One thing I forgot to mention though, the job was all done by hand and was back breakin' hard graft.

I work with a great set of lads, we call each other worse than shit, it's great crack.

The wagon heads up North, huggin' the rugged coastline. A Land steeped in a violent and bloody History. Saxon, Roman, Viking, Norman and Celtic Mysticism around every corner. Me heart is pumpin' and almost burstin' with joy...'cos by Christ I love this bloody place.

As the Arc of the Sun rises outa' the Ocean, flooding it's rays across a heaving North Sea.
At the top of me voice I sang, *"Oh what a beautiful Mornin'..."*, 'cause it was just that alright. *"Oh what a beautiful Day..."*

A grand day for graft. *"I've gorra wonderful feelin'..."* was in me prime an' glad to be alive.

The Sun rose fast now, only just below the horizon.

Soft diggin'............a good straight run.....nowt in the way. *"Everytin's goin' my wa-a-y!!!"*

The Suns on me back now, I'm pumped up & stripped to the waist. Flat out & in me stride. There's no stoppin' us now. Ha! Money for nowt. I tore into the ground.

Head down, arse up....so I didn't see it at first....and it wasn't hard to miss. It just sort of popped up from outa nowhere, sort of materialised if you like. *"Bejeezus, willyer look at that now."* Arkie saw it first and warned............"*tis a bad Omen."*

Arkie or Arkle, was named after the Legendary race horse. His Fatha was on a lucky streak at the time. Lucky for Arkie his Fatha hadn't bet on Red Rum. *"tis an amazin' t'ing.."* Arkie announced in awe as he stared up at the colossal standing stones, outlined dark silhouetted against a sheet of azure blue sky.

By Christ I was wrong about nowt being in the way.

When black Mick yelled, *"Fugg-in' 'ell."*

I had to laugh and yelled over, *"Aa bloody hope so 'cause Hell is where 'am sure to end up."*

Mick's nickname Black was a bit of a joke, 'cause his hair was pure white, but he'd dye it jet black. Mick's hair turned white with fright when he'd gone through a high tension cable with a pneumatic Jack-hammer.

The 66,000 Volts melted Mick's Wellie's and perished his elastic braces. Mick's bollocks made *'The News of the World'* and his arse *'The Sunday Sun'*. I suppose it was whichever way they wanted to look at it.

The fear was such that Mick leapt out'a his trench like Springheel Jack.

"So warra have you hit now?" The Big Fella yelled...

"You walking disaster!!"

I had to laugh, The Big Fella was the Ganger-Man, only because, no one else was daft enough to Volunteer. In theory he was the man in charge, the truth was we all knew the job off by heart. Six feet & nine inches in his bare feet...........seven feet in his size eighteen boots, thick with clarts.

He looked like Frankenstein's monster, only more ugly. Hard as nails, scared of nowt.....He'd never admit that the bloody ancient stone circle gave him the creeps. When he looked down Mick's trench, it only added to his fear.

"Bloody Hell....who the Fugg's that?" He said shaking his head.

"'tis the bloody Devil Himself." Answered Mick.

"Didn't I warn yer." Arkie preached. *"We shouldn't have dug across 'dis accursed place....we'll regret it 'til our dying days....if we live's that long."*

"'twas the shortest route.." The Big 'un said in defence.

"Bejeezus. 'tis un-holy ground." Arkie warned. *"No good will come out of this 'am tellin' yer."*

"The same as that.." Mick agreed. *"Saints forgive us!!"*

"Too true...too bloody true." Said The Murphy.

"Bollocks!!" Snarled The Big Fella.

"Double Bollock's with Knobs on." I hear meself saying an' tellin' meself *"Me 'am not superstitious...naw...'am not."* Then why was I hawkin' an spittin', and touching wood.

"Makes yer wonder don't it." Arkie said, what we were all thinking. *"Why do you suppose the only good diggin' was straight as a die, across the centre of the ring of the standin' stones."*

"What you mean? Boyo!" The Big 'un wanted to know.

"Yeah.." Arkie nodded his head. *"'tis an amazing and mysterious t'ing. 'tis as if some un-known force had a hand in it."*

"Make some sense Man!!.....Yer talkin' shite....." Big 'un snarled.

"Will yer listen man, You knows fine well what 'am sayin'." Arkie replied.

The Big fella winged on, *"Not at all."* ...He lied... *"Jesus Christ Arkie, Aa' cannit read yer bloody mind."*

It seemed that Arkie could read his and swallowed hard before he spoke......*"Dem Supernatural powers..."* He almost whispered, as if afraid to be heard.

◉ Maybe Arkie was right, I dunno, but, me, I couldn't help thinkin'.....Had the fella lay undisturbed for thousands of years.....just waiting, biding his time for the likes of us to come along and dig him up.

179

"Aye," I had to admit.... *"Spooky innit, sort of trapped in time."*

"Wat – ch – er mean?......trapped in time." The Big Fella asked, genuinely puzzled.

"The strange thing is," I told him and threw a glance at each stone in the circle as I slowly turned..... *"I've just noticed, there's twelve stones in the circle. The same as the numbers in a clock. I reckon this here could be one great big time piece."*

"an how would it work?" Murphy asked.... *"It ain't got no pointers!"*

"The Sun." I said without thinking.

"Like a sun-dial?" Arkie answered for all of us.

"Whey aye man.........the Sun." I yelled.

"'tis the Divil's clock." Mick told himself.

'An' what's that supposed to mean?...You freekin eedjit." The Big Fella asked.

"Dunno?" replied Mick.... *"Just came into me head."*

"If time waits for no one, how the fugg was it waitin' for us?" I laughed.

"Destiny they calls it." Murphy responded.

"Smash the Bugga up!!!"...Was The Big Fella's reply...that was his answer to everything. But what can you expect from a man that answers most arguments with his fists.

"Like it yes or no, the fact is 'tis an ancient relic." Arkie stated.

"So?" The Big Fella queried.

"Well wouldn't it be sacrilegious, an act of pure blasphemy to destroy such a t'ing."

Down on his hunches Mick eyes up the situation.

"Mmmmm...." Mick mumbled. *"Right Ho now."* He said to himself.

"'tis a simple task, I'll undermine the bugga...Oh yes I will." ...He agreed with himself.

Swinging the pick over his head, Mick rocked back on his heels. The Pick came down like a pile – driver.

"Aaarrgghh!!" Yelled Mick as the pick bounced back off the granite like rock.

"B – B – Bastard." Mick named the rock.

Murphy spat on his meaty hands and rubbed them together and grabbed hold of the graft.

"I'll go around the prig." He told himself.

Taking a deep breath he drove the spit hard into the wall of the trench.

"Ooouucchh!!" Bellowed Murphy as the graftin' tool stotted off the wall of rock with a Cunk!!......almost shattering his wrists.

It was now pretty obvious that we needed a jack hammer.

"Go over the prig!!"...someone uttered half hearted...however, a blind man could see that it wasn't deep enough.

There was only one thing for it, we'd have to lift the bugga out. Grabbin' the length of rope I dived down Mick's trench. I had to laugh at my theory about it being a ship's figure head. It would have sunk the ship....it weighed a bloody ton.

"When yer ready boys." The Big Fella ordered...*"On the hup – hya –hya – hup!!!"* We heaved with all our might on the end of the rope.

"Now ain't he somethin' to be lookin' at." Arkie said as he looked sideways at the statue, with the eye of an artist.

"It's bloody great." Uttered the Murphy.

"Ain't it grand??" exclaimed Mick.

"Yer right there." Even The Big 'Un had to agree.

> ▣ The boys ooohhdd & aaaahhdd in wonderment as I went down on me knee's to take a better look at whatever it was. Arkie was right about one thing. Him or it, was certainly somethin' to look at. The detail was amazin', it's paintwork un-blemished. He wore chain-mail and a breast-plate with either a sea serpent or a dragon emblazoned on it. His steel gauntlets gripped a mighty broad sword. A strong proud face with piercing sea green eye's that seemed to look through you.

"Bbrrrr..." I shuddered as if somebody had just walked over me grave.

"Ain't that a crown on his head?" Mick said.

"Yeah..." the Big Fella Agreed,.." *'e must have been a king."*

"Or a Saint." Says Murphy, *"Sure, that could well be a Halo."*
"Or maybe both." Arkie said with the passion of a poet. *"Most likely one of yer true heroes. The stuff of legends."*

"Ha!!" I had to laugh...*"Make yer bloody minds up...The fella was a Devil down a black hole, now he's a Saint in the cold light of day."* I finished.
"Maybe yes an' maybe no." Replied Arkie, shaking his head and scratching his chin....
"I'll not be arguing wit'cher. But one things for certain, whoever yer man was or might have been. The fact is he must have been pretty important for himself to be buried slap bang in the centre of this ancient stone circle."

"What-cha mean?" I argued...*"Callin' it him?......it's a bloody stone statue man. It ain't real, it ain't flesh and blood. It never was...well was it?"*

The Big Fella massaged his huge chin as he examined the face of the statue.
"Aaah." He growled, shaking his head...*"Now there's where you'd be wrong Boyo."*
"An' how would You known?...How can anyone ever know?" I questioned.
"May be yes an' maybe no, all I know for sure, yer man's true likeness has been chizzled outa this iron – hard, livin' rock.......it'll last for eternity." The Big Fella shrugged and waved his huge hands as he spoke. He'd an awful habit of talkin' with his hands. An' if you didn't listen, he'd talk with his fists.

"The t'ing is..." Mick said as a matter of factly...*"Whoever he was, he's in the bloody way."*
"Yer right there Micky lad. An' I'll tellyer summit for nowt. We'd better get rid of Him whoever he is...an' sharpish like before 'em Archeologist fella's get wind of it. They'll be here in their droves, like flies around a dung heap." I replied.

The Big Fellas face turned white.

"Don't suppose you can remember Durham?...can Yer?" I reminded him.

The Big Fella's face contorted like he was being tortured...*"I do."* He said.
"Mind that was a great picture of you at the time. Holding 'em great big bones." I stated.
"Now don't be talkin' about that now." He cringed at the memory

"Made most of the papers. Front page of The Daily Mirror. What was the head lines again...?" I continued.

"Will yer shut the fugg up.." The Big Un growled.

"Whey aye....i remember now..." me again.

"Geordie.....I'm warnin' yer now.." The Big Fella was roused.

"NAAVY – DIGS, UP – DONKEY – SAURUS – REX..."....I stated.

I Ducked as a huge right fist went sailin' over me head.

"I'll tell yer somethin' for nowt. It would never have made the front page if them Dinosaur bones hadn't turned out to be some owld Donkey's." I ended.

"We'll be havin' no more of them shenanigans, Yer gob shite!" The Big Fella winged.

"But surely." Arkie begged..*"This is different."*

"How's it different?" Snorted The Big Un.

Arkie hesitated as he searched for the right words...

"Unique!" He sighed, *"Yeah it is unique."*

"Unique...my arse." The Big Fella growled.

"Now Yer talkin'..." I Joked, *"Yer always talking out'a yer arse."*

"Will Yer hush..." Arkie pleaded...*"'tis no joking matter..'tis an ancient Relic of great importance."*

"'an how would you know that?" I asked.

"Anyhow.." Says the Big Fella..*"If 'em orch-ee-ol-igee ...fella's come...and they surely will. The job will be stopped for sure."*

We all agreed on that..................

"So right yer are boy's" The Big Fella continued....

"'tis back to square one..all in favour of smashin' the brute up, raise yer hands."

"All those against...raise Yer feet." I sarcastically said.

Arkie was the only one who didn't raise his hand....Oh and The Murphy, *"Ar..yes..no..yes..no.."* He could never make up his mind.

The daft sod ended up flat on his back, with both arms and both legs raised. *"We'll take that as a no vote...yi daft bugga."* I laughed.

"I really don't know meself." Answered The Murphy.

183

At least he was honest, who ever really knows 'emselves.

The Big fellow was over the moon. Now all he had to do was smash the bugger up an' get rid of it.
The sooner the better.

"All right now." He said to himself. His long thick fingers curled around the heavy hammers shaft, like a bunch of banana's. Gasping a huge lung full of air, he swung the hammer way up and over his shoulder, arching his narrow back....like a fully drawn longbow.

"Whooopeee!!!" He Yelled, before he brought the mighty – mell down...like a pile driver.

We all tensed waiting for the smack...but didn't expect a "BOOM!!" and a *FLASH*, that almost knocked us on our backs.

"OOYYAAH!!" The Big Fella Shouted as the force of the explosion launched him backwards..still grippin' the hammer. In a blurred cartwheel, of head and heels, he flew arse over tits.

We looked on in amazement, overcome by the splendour of the achievement...Naw, I'm lying...we laughed 'til we cried.

"Yer made a right arse outa that." Said Mick as the Big Fella struggled drunkenly to his feet. Mick winked as he continued.. *"'twas a great backwards sommer sault..can't argue with that...but I can only give yer marks...9 outa 10....was yer landin' that let yer down."*

The Big Fella composed himself and went on to say, *"Everyone of you are a lot of piss takin' bastards...an' whoever the statue was....is a shit house bastard."* ...dropping his voice into almost a whisper as he went on to say, *"As sure as god is my witness...dat..'ting"* ....pointing a shaky finger towards the statue... *"Is possessed."*...he lifted his beloved hammer...

"Will you look at the state of that."...he exclaimed as he juggled the hammer head from hand to hand...like a hot potato.

"Jesus Christ." Uttered Mick in amazement.

"God Almighty." Said Murphy.

"Holy Mother of God." Arkie added as he crossed himself.

"Whey yer Bugga." Says I.

The Hammer head was twisted and mis-shapened, as if it had been melted by some terrific heat.....like a meteorite and it was still smouldering. The Shaft...well what was left of the shaft, was pure charcoal....burnt to a crisp.

"By Christ.." I Joked and nodded at The Big Fella, *"You looked for all the World like that Fella...whats 'is name....Thor!..The Viking God of Thunder."*

"Who the fugg's Thor, when he's at home?" Asked Murphy.

He'd no sooner got the words out of his mouth........when..BOOM!!!...a loud clap of Thunder clapped in the distance and a jagged fork of lightning came right on cue. The Big Fella jumped and nearly crapped himself...and by the look on his face, just maybe he had.

"If yer ask me, let's dump the bugga." I suggested.

"Bloody great idea that..." The Big Fella nodded his head..."But where?"

"I don't know myself." ...Said The Murphy to himself..."What would You do?"

"Who...Me??" They all looked at me.

"Ahr there's yer answer." I says sniffin' the salt sea air...

"It's up to yersell's, but ain't a burial in the deep blue sea far better than a mucky hole in the ground."

"Too true." The Big Fella agreed.

All bar Arkie nodded their heads in agreement.

"You'll regret it 'til yer dyin' day.....if yer live that long." Arkie declared.

"Ha!!"...I laughed.."Roll on death an' giz a rest."

"Yer askin' for trouble." Arkie warned.

"C'mon now....Me askin' for trouble. Don't make me laugh....Makes a change. Ain't it the other way round...............Trouble had an awful habit of askin' after me."

"All together boys."............The Big Un hollered..."*Ready – Steady – Heeaa-ve!!*"

As one we heaved the statue, like a coffin. Up and on to our shoulders.

"By the left...........quick march.." I prompted......it did make sense to keep in step over the rough ground.

- ▣ The moment we stepped outside the stone circle, the temperature dropped and the sky looked menacing. A sudden wind came up, charging, howling from the direction of the sea. In the distance, a terrible thunderstorm was brewing.

- ▣ On un-even legs, with leaden feet we strode out a slow death march. Up a slope, leaning into the wind, over a wild and rugged landscape. Clouds rolled towards us like great black boulders, tumbling down a purple-black mountainside. Sparks of lightning flash all around us like an artillery barrage. A jet black silhouette of a ruined castle broken towers seemed to reach up and grab hold of the clouds. On we marched. Like shell shocked, half dead soldiers over no-mans land towards the roar of the guns in the distance. Or was it the roaring and the booming of an angry sea. Nothing seemed real. I half expected to come under attack at any moment and jumped....we all did when an ear bursting clap of thunder rattled our bones. A bright jagged sword of lightning flashed and flared....lighting this place in a ghostly glow.

- ▣ And the rain came...just like we knew it would. Drops of rain splattered down, stottin' off my head like a drum roll. By Christ it was hard goin'...i'm bloody knackered. My feet are heavy and awkward now as the wind clasps a freezing hand over me mouth an' nose....robbin' me of breath. An' just when the claggy – clarts threaten to suck the boots off me sodden feet, the mud gave way to rock beneath our swellchin' boots.

▣ Soaked to the skin and chilled to the bone, we finally reach our destination. Exhausted, panting and heaving for breath. For all the world, looking like a bunch of washed-up shipwrecked sailors. We gaze out over the heaving sea. A torrent of rain drives down so hard that I'm gulping and breathin' rain.

"Jesus Christ...........im drownin'.."
I'm scared shitless now but daresn't show it. Even hard cases are scared of the unknown. It's like the end of the world.
In less than a heart beat me life flashes before me.......guess I didn't have much of a life. I force out a laugh that comes out like a cry and nearly chokes meself.
Me hearts pounding like a drum...
"What the fuck's gannin' on?" ...I shout as the rain and wind stops as suddenly as it came.

Then this strange voice is telling me...

"THY WIND OF PROPHECY HATH AROSE....
...HERALDING THIS WARRIOR FROM PLACE OF BRIEF REST."

By Christ I'm hearing voices now.
"I VOW THOU ART THE CHOSEN ONE...."

""Who me....hu!!.....chosen one me arse." I blurt out.

"TAKE HEED, YE WHO HEAVED ME FROM A PLACE OF DARKNESS TO A PLACE OF LIGHT."...the voice boomed.

"I only tied the bloody rope man!!!" I shout.

"HENCE FROM DEATH TO LIGHT,,,THUS LION AWAKES. ETERNAL THANKS TO THEE OH NOBLEST OF ALL HEROES..."

"Oh it was nowt really man, just forget about it."...Christ I'm talkin' to meself...they'll come an' take me away.

187

"I CRAVE THEE WILL FOLLOW ME UPON THIS HOLIEST OF QUESTS."
"Naw.....don't bloody well think so."

"COME HITHER MY GOOD FELLOW...THOU WILL NOT REFUSE ME!!"

"Had-a-way to hell." ...I yell.

Me fatha was right... *"Too many cracks on your heed and you'll end up daft!!"* he often told me...if he was alive today, he'd turn over in his grave.

"ME THINKS THOU DOTH FALSEHOOD BY ME....RELENT OR I SHALL TEAR OPEN THE LONG HIDDEN WOUNDS IN THY PRESENCE AND BLEED THE NOBLEST OF BLOOD.."

We've got a right bulls knacker here I'm thinkin'....or could it be that somebody's throwin' their voice at the statue like one of 'em ventriloquist dummies... *"Whey-aye man.."*
I say convincing meself that it's one of the boys is takin' the piss....but, I only half believed it.

"HASTEN, COME MY GOOD FELLOW, FOLLOW ME ON THE HOLIEST OF QUESTS. WE FEW, WE HAPPY FEW, THE BAND OF BROTHERS."

I think he wants me and the lad's to join the sally-army band.

"FOR HE TODAY, THAT SHEDS HIS BLOOD WITH ME. SHALL FOREVER BE MY BROTHER."

"Sorry mate, if it's blood donors yer after you've no chance here....only last week I gave me pint of claret at the hospital."

An' when the voice ranted and raved,
"IN THE NAME OF GOD, THIS MUST BE THE MOST HOLIEST OF ERRANDS..."
Well it would be...wouldn't it.

"...HASTEN...COME NOW GOOD FELLOW."
He could talk a glass eye to sleep, this one could.

"ME THINKS THOU WILL NOT REFUSE ME."
I'm thinkin' he's gotta be one of them bloody Jehouva's witnesses...enough was enough. An' when he shouts...

"FOR SAINT GEORGE AND MERRY ENGLAND....."

That was when we launched the barmy bugga over the cliff. Up and away it flew, we didn't known our own strength.
Entering the water, it was gone.....without hardly a splash.

Then silence..total silence, it was as if time had suddenly stopped.

"Good riddance." Uttered the Murphy.
"Yer right there." Agreed Mick.
"Thank God." Says The Big Fella.

Arkie crossed himself and said something in Latin...or it might have been Gaelic. Anyway, whatever it was, it was supposed to ward off the evil spirits. I had a feeling that it wasn't going to work.

Another storm was coming in fast. The clouds much bigger and darker than before. I could hear my heart thumpin' like a drum. I daresn't breath... as I stared wide eyed at the menacing volcanic clouds rolling and tumbling over the surf skimmed sea.

It came towards the shore....just like we knew it would.

> Giant waves roaring and crashing against the rocks like the roar of gunfire before an attack. We watch the storm with a fearful fascination. Paralysed...we stood like statues on a war memorial, our feet cemented to the rock. Our fear turned to deep excitement, it was if we were witnessing The Creation itself.

The rain came on softly and then began to drive hard. In seconds it became ferocious with musket ball sized hail stones. In the distance bursts of thunder sounded...the clouds shatter, bursting overhead.

This was unreal, the sky had become an immense dark whirlpool that crashed and quaked with the roar of thunder.

"Bob..bloody Hell's flames." Someone stammered....he wasn't far off the truth.

Trunks of lightning forked their way down to the ground all around us... seeming to reach the very depths of Hell.

"Jesus Christ!!!" I yelled... *"The whole bloody world is shakin'.."* I grimaced and yelled louder.. *"God help us."*

"Aaah com'on now, don't you be talkin' to God yer bloody heathen." Arkie mocked.

"Gods got a good mind to send down a couple of bolts of lightning to strike yerself down stone dead....An' here's me standing a little bit too close for comfort."

Right on cue, a couple of balls of ground lightning came rollin' towards us, skipping and flaring over the sea. Like drops of cold water hitting a hot frying pan. It sizzled, jumped and crackled as it came.

What could I do?...I did what most atheist's do, when they think they're about to leave this world. I says me bloody prayers.

"Jesus!!!"...I shout....as I fight the urge to lift my hands over my eyes....to shut out what's gonna blast me too Hell...or Kingdom Come.

A strange eerie feeling is deep inside me and the hair on my head jumps straight on end....just before an almighty...CCRR – AAA – AA – CCKKK!!! Lightning's fatal blow. There's a fierce white hot burning.

A blue yellow bolt of lighting struck me in the chest. Me skin tingled with pins and needles.

I feel me-self lifting, hovering...me burnt out boots dangling above the ground.

An' am saying........*"Am floatin'.............am a ghost...Bloody Hell man, is a dead?"*

If I was, an' I might well have been...natures elements sharp brought me back to life. The sky opens up and a torrent of ice cold rain drives me down to earth. A wonderful feeling of pure tranquillity is in me now, taking possession of my body and soul.

There's this strange shimmering blue light all around us now like the moon's crescent......

And I'm hearing voices again.

"I THANK YEE AND BEFORE I DEPART...I DUB THEE THE NOBLEST OF KNIGHTS. SIR GEORDIE, WHAT SAYETH THEE."

"So what the Hell, gan on then. But gan canny with that sword or you'll have my head off!!"

"FARE THY WELL   ..." The voice echoed as if down a well...**"I MUST AWAY.."**

And I'm laughing at meself, as lunatics do.

Nowt makes any sense at all. Me Mothers voice in me head is sayin',
"Too many cracks on the heed wor Georgie, will knock Yer daft."

The sun burst's through a hole in the middle of the clouds. It's spotlight beam reflecting a blinding needle of silver light.....and as if by magic, the sea went calm, not a wave.....only a ring of ripples on the water. In the centre of the ring, a gauntleted fist wields a broadsword. It's silver blade glistening in a magical shimmering glow.

An' me fatha's voice echoes in me skull.
"Yer live in a bloody dream world. I'll bloody well knock some sense into you."

My head is pounding, me head is hurting, me head is bursting as he hit's me again an' again.

When I was a kid – only me dreams kept me sane.

"Excalibur." I said and wasn't afraid to be heard.
"What-cher-on about?" Black Mick's voice broke the spell... *"What the fugg's Excalibur?"*

Thank God I was alive an' kicking.

"Yer a bloody head case." Murphy followed.

Yes, I was back in the real world.

*"Where the hell have yer been?"...*The Big Un yelled...

"You barmy coont, playin' hide an' seek."

"Anyway, yer didn't answer me question." Say's Mick...

"What the fugg's Excalibur?"

"King Arthur man, Excalibur...was his sword, a magical sword." I replied.

"Arffur, Who?" Murphy scoffed..."*C'mon now, yer makin' it up, yer takin' the piss, well ain't yer now."*

"Naw, King Arthur Pendragon man." I stated.

"Alright, so wouldn't he be the fella who went an' killed the dragon?" The Big Fella chimmed in.

"Naw man,.." I tied to explain,..."*The King Arthur an' the Knight's of the round table."...*

"Camalot, Lady Guenivere, Lancelot an' that." Arkie recited.

"Oh I see." Say's the Murphy.."*Who Killed The Dragon then?"*

"Murphy?" I said.

"Yeah." He answered.

"Fuck the Dragon!!"

The sword was fast disappearing in a sudden shroud of Sea mist...then it was gone. If they'd seen it, they never let on.

....

"Will Yer take a look at that now." Murphy said all excited.

"Bejeezus, now how would that happen now?" The Big Fella gasped.

"If Yer ask me, it's gorra be a miracle." Said Mick...crossing himself.

"Amazin'." Added Arkie...flabbergasted.

An' when Murphy cried, *"Now yer wouldn't t'ink that would happen. Holy mother of God....now would Yer."*

I thought to meself they'd actually seen something after all, but naw, I was the only one looking out to sea.

The rest of them had their thick heads together......ooohin' and aaahin'... looking googily eyed at the miracle........that was Murphy's owld watch.

The same watch that had stopped going over thirty years ago. It was now ticking away like a time bomb.

Strange.....aye, can't argue with that. But hardly a bloody miracle. Maybe so, but what was even harder to explain and beyond belief. The one handed time piece, had only went and grew another hand. It was a bit ironic I suppose. I'd laughed at the lads, now they were laughing at me...They'd had their little miracle..............and excalibur was one big joke.......sunk without a trace. I didn't want to spoil it for them now, did I.........I tell a lie, why – aye, I certainly did.

"Now just you's had Yer horses.." I said with sarcasm.

"Before you's happy band of barmy buggas phone the Vatican and ask the Pope to declare Murphy a Saint, I've been thinking.........i reckon there's always been a couple of pointers on Murphys' Grandfatha's owld watch."

"Oh no there bloody ain't." argued Murphy.

"What Yer on about." Arkie jumped to Murphy's defence.

"Well use yer loaf, think about it man." I said.

Murphy thought long and hard about it but was none the wiser, so I took it on meself to explain.

"It's simple man, stands to bloody reason. One pointer was hidden away behind the other. It had to be, and when the watch began to work again...naturally they moved apart. Well didn't they? ..Stands to reason, don't it."

"Bejeezus boy, aren't you the clever one." Arkie said more in anger than amazement. He was in the huff, like a little kid who'd just had his balloon burst.

"Explain," asked Mick, *"If yer can Yer clever coont. Why would a watch that had been stopped for all this time, would suddenly take it on itself to start tickin' away again."*

There was a long pause as I tried to get me head around it.

Murphy jumped in, *"Are – so, Yer don't know now do you, gob –shite."*

Murphy was full of hell alright, this was pretty personal. The watch was like a family heirloom, a talisman, bore like a medal with pride. The owld watch had stopped the same moment his granda's heart had stopped.

Now it were going again, were the dead tryin' to say somethin'.

Murphy would like to believe they were.

"'tis a mysterious an' wonderful t'ing." Murphy muttered to himself, with his ear to the watch.

Who was I to disillusion 'em. Let 'em believe in their little miracle. Like I say's, I'm no killjoy, naw I definitely wasn't.

But Arkie looked me in the eye as if he could see right through me.

"Now then," he smirked, *"admit yer wrong."*

"Well I suppose..." Didn't finish me sentence.

It was Murphys over the top, sarcastic laugh that made me change my mind.

"It's simple man, when yer think about it....ain't hard to fathom out." I continued. Arkie shrugged his shoulders.

"Well it is isn't it..." I said louder this time.

Murphy stopped the laughing and they all looked blank.

So I went on...

"Well did you ever see that great owld horror picture...Frankenstein?"

They all nodded, which I took to sayin' that they had.

"Alright, so to cut a long story short, remember what brought the Monster to life."

I started.

Still silence.................

"So you don't remember then?...well I'll give you's a clue – in fact I'll give you's a couple of clues right. A BOOM and a FLASH., made the spark that started the monsters heart beating." ...I exclaimed.

"It wouldn't be thunder and lightning, now would it." Says Mick.

"That it would." I Joked, *"Give the monkey a banana."*

"So?" Mick questioned.

"So, it's simple man. It was the thunder and lightning which started the watch tickin'." I stated.

"What thunder and lightning?..." The Big Fella repeated...

"Had – a – way to hell, Yer pullin' me leg. That bloody thunder storm would have wakened the dead." I protested.

"An' what storm would that be now?" Murphy asked.

I knew for a fact that Murphy wasn't lying.......he wouldn't know how to.

....

Belchin' a thick blue cloud of Diesel smoke, the open back wagon thunders straight as a die, down the old Roman Road, heading back home. Fightin' to keep me eye's open, I gaze hypnotized at the moon, as it bounces along in pace with us.

Murphy's voice booms from outa' the back, *"Bejeezus, now yer wouldn't t'ink it was that time already now would yer."*

The moons lunatic face is grinning down at us. An' I have to laugh, 'cause it's a fact, the moon's gorra good right to laugh ...'cause Murphy's owld watch ain't just a tick – a – tickin' along....naw!, it's now totally indestructible, shock proof, water proof, fire proof and Murphy proof. An' even better than that can yer believe, it's face ain't just illuminous. It's better than that man. It's face sparkles and shimmers, brighter than the brightest of stars. An' I swear to God that this is no word of a lie.......the owld watch talks to Murphy.
"Six o'clock..." We hear... *"Bejeezus, now you wouldn't think it was that* time *would yer now."*..the watch say's to Murphy.
"No yer wouldn't.." The Murphy answers back.

An' owld Murphy smiles away to himself 'cause now he'll never need to learn to tell the time.....Naaw!...not now he don't, now that the time tells him.

I have to laugh as I stare outa' the back of the open wagon as it thunders it's way along the old Roman Road, straight as a die headin' for home. I'm laughin' all the way and dreamin' sweet dreams with me eyes wide open....

THE END

A Miracle ....

Maybe...........................

"THE LAST NAVVY."

We passed the cap for owld Patsy O'Reilly the other day.
Did I say owld?...By Christ, the owld bugger wasn't nearly as owld as mesel'..!

Death's a fact of life, can't argue with that. Even so, I'll tell you summat for nowt. They say it was his heart.....had-a-way to Hell!!
I know different...it was hard graft that finally put O'Reilly in the ground.
All the same, didn' the pick a daft time to be planted, the awkward owld sod!! Can yer believe it?....New Years Bloody Eve!!

Anyway, there was a right good turn out for the occasion, all the young bucks were there. Must admit, I felt a bit strange, a bit out of place....like as though I was sort of on a different wavelength.
All the owld faces were missing, but after a couple of pints I started to unwind. Relax in the company like.
All the young 'uns took their turn to come over and shake me hand and have a bit of crack. I suppose I was a bit of a father figure, having worked with their Dads.

So we gave Owld Patsy a great send-off.
Naturally, we spoke a lot about O'Reilly, well at least I did most of the talking. It's not that I like the sound of me own voice, naw, it wasn't that. Yer see, me an' him belonged to the same generation, a different world from today. So anyway, it was left to me to say a few words. I tells them what a great fella he was....which he wasn't.
But still, it's bad crack to speak ill of the dead.

Must admit, the drink loosened me tongue and I went a bit over the top when I asked them, "***How is it, when a man has just learned about life and how to live.......it's time to die?***"

I spoke of the past and days that are long gone. As I told the tale, I gazed around at me captive audience, taking in all the faces. It was only then that it hit me, by Christ it made me feel really owld, 'cause I hadn't just worked

197

with most of their Dads, I also worked with a couple of their Granda's as well. And that's when I'm thinkin'......with O' Reilly gone' it makes me the last man of the owld gang.

Funny how you never feel any owlder than the men you're workin' with, ...don't matter how owld you are, you're always thinkin' of yoursel' as one of the boys.

Normally I don't talk about mortality, but lately I've been thinkin' about it. It's a fact of life isn't it, especially when one of me owld mates pops his clogs. One of these days it'll be my turn for the cap to be passed around. Wonder how much these greedy bastards will cough-up?
I've a bloody good mind to ask for me nobbin' right now, so's I can enjoy it...have a drink on mesel'...so to speak. When me time comes, who'll stand up and' say a few words over me. Every bugger's dead that knows us!! Will any of these young 'uns remember me.......i doubt it. To them, I'm just a miserable owld sod, always whinging on about the owld days.

Aye, maybe I do....but the young 'uns don't really know me. In fact when I comes to think about it, I hardly know mesel'!! But at times like these, I can so easy let mesel' go and drift away on a mental tide into the past, all the memories come flooding back as plain as day...I can remember everything...

....

I came into the world in 1939 and me Da' joked at the time.....
"By the state of his face, the midwife didn't just smack his arse, she gave him a bloody good hiding!!"

Ma', God rest her soul, reckoned there was a bit of a mix-up in the maternity ward the day I was born. Ma' had been over three hours in labour and went through seven sorts of hell. When the baby finally arrived, kickin' and screamin', Ma' didn't see it...she was out for the count. When she finally opened her eyes, all the hurt and pain were instantly forgotten, when the most beautiful little baby girl was placed gently into her mothers arms.

"Eee, what a bonny; little bairn!!"

Ma' had just enough time to say, before the new love of her life was snatched away. In it's place they plonked me.

Poor Ma' must have got the fright of her life, she'd lost an Angel and gained a hairless Chimpanzee!!

She screamed blue bloody murder. And who can blame her, the shock of seein' my ugly mug grinnin' toothlessly up at her was enough to send poor Ma' into orbit. When she came down, she wasn't over happy...

"It's bloody horrible!!" she yelled.

"Take it away an' give it a bloody banana!!" she screamed...before firing me like a cannon-ball into the beside cot.

Aye, she was a carin' and sensitive old Lady, me Ma'.

Da' said, *"If yer face was yer fortune, yer'd die with hunger!!"*

There was no arguin' with that. Even so, ma', God love her, breast-fed me in the air-raid shelter while owld Adolf dropped his bombs on Byker.

I'm sure that lookin' 'down, in his wisdom must have said to himself,-

"I'd better give that ugly kid a bloody good sense of humour, he's certainly goin' to need it!!"

Because I remember, that over the years, the older I got, the more I learnt to laugh at life....sometimes at others, but mostly at meself. Laughter became my religion, out of which an inner strength grew with time.

....

........Young Malloy started singing'....

"On Mother Kelly's doorstep...."

Everyone joined in. It's one of those songs that always takes me back to the time when I was a kid. We had nowt, yet we had everything. We knew no other.

▣   Belchin' chimneys were our skyline, cobbled lanes were our playground. On bombed sites we played soldiers, throwin' hand-grenades at Fat-Joe, a German Tiger Tank, and shot down Lanky Billy Robson, a Stuka Dive-Bomber. At the deadly sound of the machinegun...a-rat-a-tat-a-tat, we dived into our trenches. Raggy-arsed and as black as coal dust, we'd run for the sake of running.

The clatter of hob-nail boots sending sparks flying. We were like shadows chasing shadows in gas-lit, slate-paved streets. The sirens sound of Mothers' voices echoing a chorus around our domain, calling us safely home, each and every one of us by first name.

▣ Clammin' with the hunger and mortally wounded we limped home from the war, singing, "**Hitler, he's only got one ball**...."

Scrubbed clean and shining, with a scaldin' cup of cocoa and jam 'n' bread, fed we'd sleep like the dead, head to toe...like sardines in a tin.

A fight starts in the corner, nobody takes any notice, it's only O'Sullivan and Black Mick. They're the best of mates, but fight each other three times a week, just for the fun of it.

Will yer look at them, both bloody useless...

"Yer couldn't fight yer way out of a wet paper bag!!", I tells them.

Aye, the drink makes yer think more clearly about the past, all them years drifting away. Seeing them two nuggets over there, takes me back to that time....was in me prime and didn't know who I was or what I wanted to be...mad at the world or was it at meself?

All that aggression I wanted to and needed to fight. The Boxers' hardest opponents are fear and self-doubt. All those doubts and fears are gone at the clang of a bell. The kill or be killed feeling that brings the adrenaline pumping through me veins and without even thinking about it, I'm dancing, keeping the weight on the balls of me feet and without even trying, I move with the grace of a cat. Bobbing and weaving, snapping out short sharp punches...faster than the eye can see.

In me minds eye, I can see myself then...looked great I did, could have been a champion!!

In their eyes now, I am what I look...a punch drunk owld fighter who led with his chin!!

Well, maybe I am, but age brings a man down off his toes. Life's one big 15 round fight and I'll go the distance as the best I can. I've learnt to pace meself....stop wading in like some punch-drunk fighter and most important of all...ride with the blows.

By Christ, I've changed over the years....had to change with the times. When I think back, I sometimes wonder if it was all a dream....if I've really been there.

Feet shuffled on the dusty floorboards, glasses clinked and smoke smarted me eyes. They spoke of football, fist fights and shaggin'...and all of the women they reckoned they'd had. I listened, nodded and smiled to my self...they were young and daft, well on their way to being owld men afore their time. But when they started braggin' about all the hard graft they'd done and how the owld timers couldn't live with the likes of them....all them owld navvies must have turned in their graves.
Somebody had to tell them...."*Hah, calls yersel's navvies, yer couldn't lace yer fatha's boots!!.......Yer can laugh.*"

And they did.....
"*Gan on then, but I tell you's summat for nowt, all the real navvies are dead an' gone, the likes of which yer'll never see again. We had no bloody diggin' machines... ... ...was all done by hand in the owld days!!*"

The Hammer …….

'BELL METAL'

And….

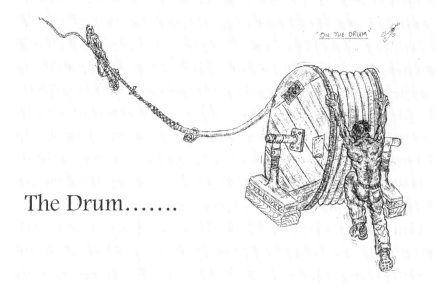

'ON THE DRUM'

The Drum…….

Somebody mimicked a melancholy violin....and I had to laugh with the young'uns.

....

Funny how when we're down we laugh at nowt, the strangest of things, the simplest of jokes, someone's funny walk...sentences that come out back-to-front, a word that comes out wrong.........
Why?...to kid ourselves, to hide the misery.........i suppose it's like whistlin' in the dark.

Could tell 'em how it was, but they don't wanna know.
They live for today and who can blame them, yer only live once an' there's nee gannin' back!!
Maybe there's a God, I don't know, would like to think there was. They reckon yer life's planned out before yer born, destiny they calls it.

Anyway, too much thinkin's bad for yer, but the owlder I get, the more I live on the memories and between you and me, when I'm drunk I can live those memories.

> ▣ On me left foot I tied me foot-iron, it's worth it's weight in gold. A line string across the fields marks the cable-run. To make top bonus, a drums length...250 Yards – 2'6" deep has to be dug out, the three and a half ton of high tension cable pulled by hand...laid off in the cut and back filled in a day............would kill a horse, but not us, we were bloody lunatics.....thought we were invincible, thought we would live forever!

I strode out a good ten yards and mark the ground with me heel...it's me first stretch of the day. We work as a gang, but dig alone, facing one another's back. It's a race, there's no denying that but the rivalry is friendly....it's always there.
Pride is at stake and I'm proud to be able to set the pace but still I'll always have doubts and wonder if I'll have the strength that will see me through the day, but hate the thought of mesel' for ever thinkin' it......snarlin' and growlin' I calls mesel' a few swear words.
The sweat will flow like rivers, smarting eyes and making underarms red-

raw. So it's stripped to the waist, take in a deep breath and I drive down hard on the graft.

Starting is always the hardest, huffin' an' puffin' like some owld steam engine. Slowly at first, strugglin' to get goin', gradually warmin' up. As the momentum builds up, change gear, breakin' into our stride, faster and faster....it's full steam ahead.
The long silver blades of the grafting tools attack the virgin ground like spears, foot-ironed boots work like pile-drivers. The clink of steel on steel echoes down the line.

They say hard graft never killed anybody....what a load of crap, we knew that, even so, we never slowed down. It's madness, but work....hard work is really like a drug, yer just can't stop yersel'.
It's a great feelin' when yer in full flow....a sense of peace flows into the mind, soul and body.
The feelin' is as near to heaven as I'll ever get, but at the same time, I knew that by the end of the day I'll feel at death's door and closer to bloody Hell!! Even so, we spat into the Devils' eye and dug ourselves into an early grave.

We'd crawl over the back of the wagon more dead than alive, yet still we'd never show it....all too proud to show we're beat.
Then the crack would flow.....

    ▣ When yer work with men and drink with them, yer really get to know them. We'd laugh at each other and call each other every name under the Sun and love every insult that was thrown our way....savour it then throw one back. Oh aye, a great bunch of boys, all gone but not forgotten...... for when I look close at the young 'uns, I can see their Father's faces and through their eyes, I'll always be one of the boys.

The last round of the Old Year becomes the first of the New...
"Cheers Mate,"......hand shakes...
"Happy New Year,"...Hugs...
"All the best,"......Back slaps...
"Be seein' yer soon mate,"...
"Aye, so long, gan canny eh!!"

Wha'rra great night, wha'rra great bloody day.....Wha'rra drink....i feel bloody mortal...No I feel bloody immortal!!

Must hurry, can't wait to get home, all the family will be up and celebrating. Waitin' for me.........Aye, just for me.

Can yer believe I've been nominated to be the first foot for the New Year, for the bloody New Millenium.
God, I feel privileged, isn't life great......ain't it just grand!!

And I'll tell yer summat for nowt, last night I was on me way out......on me last legs.
Today I'm up on me toes again.............ready to take on the Bloody World again.

Why?..........'cause I'm one of the boys again, one of the gang!!

Oh aye, I'm a new man......a new Millenium Man!!!!!

THE END

END OF

PART TWO

The Last Navvy

◉ *PART THREE*

And The Blossom Fell

The Big Eat

"THE BIG EAT."

Regular as clock-work.

You could set your watch by them.

12 O'clock on the dot, they walked into Peters' Bar.

Big Davey first......with little Tucker in tow.

Peter pulled two pints of Scotch without being told.

Davey was as big and jolly.....as Tucker was miserable and small.

"Yer beer's like piss!!" Tucker moaned even before Peter had finished drawing the draught from the pumps.

It was water off a ducks back to Peter.

"The day owld misery guts smiles," Peter said to himself... *"Pigs'll fly!!"*

Everybody was Daveys' friend. Tucker only had the two....that's if you could call Davey his friend.

They'd known each other since they were bairns, I'd yet to hear him say a kind word to big Davey...in fact he called him worse than shit!!

But Davey didn't seem to mind, he gave as good as he got.

"Git the bugga doon yer throat, yer miserable little shit." Say's Davey...

Swallowing his pint in one gulp.

Tucker never married...

"Nee bugga would have him." According to Big Davey.

Tuckers' other pal, Henry...was the only fella he seemed to care about. Some said this phantom friend of his was a figment of his imagination... nobody had laid eyes on him.

"Same again." Says Davey, smacking his lips.

"An' the same for me little pal here...alright Tucker me little mate!!"

Davey said, slapping Tucker on his back......nearly sending him to his knees.

"Will Yer bloody give owa-man!!" Tucker groaned.

"Why do yer hev ti....dee that, yer big daft bugga. Divin't yer know, that it bloodywell hurts."

"Sorry mate......drink up, Might cheer yer up a bit.....Owld misery guts." Says Davey between large gulps of beer.

"The trouble with you, is yer divvent know yer own strength man!!" Tucker continued.

"I says A'm sorry..." Davey pleaded...... *"Didn't I!!"*

"Yer always bloody sorry." Tucker told him and headed for the free grub on the counter.

"Aa keep hoping....." Davey complained as he joined Tucker at the counter... *"One of these days, yer ganna hev some proper grub on this counter..... like tripe an' black pudding, instead of cheese and celery...yuk!!....i'm a meat man me. Anyway, giz another pint....it's your turn short-arse."*

Peter looked up with a mouthful of cheese... *"Huh!!"* Says he.
"Will yer listen to him...Desperate Dan.....what-cher want for nowt man..... bloody cow pie!!"

"Huh!!....if yer were hungry, yer'd eat owt.." Said Tucker munching on a stick of celery.

"Look..." says Davey... *"I'm very particular what I put inside of me. A man needs proper grub."*

"That's all you ever think about....is yer stomach....yer always bragging about how much yer can eat." Tucker told him.

"Aye, that's me alright, drink an' eat any man under the table...eat a scabby horse me..." Davey laughed....
"An' swill it down with a barrel of beer."......
Davey laughed even harder and slapped his beer belly with both hands.

"Daft as a brush." Muttered Tucker, nodding his head...
"Daft as a bloody brush yer big fat sod."

Davey did a little jig and wiggled his hips.

"I'd like you to know....That in my younger days, they used to call me snake-hips. "....replied Davey.

Tucker sniggered and eyed Davey's belly.

"Aye..." says Tucker....
"Aa can believe that yer went an' swallowed a whole pig."

Everyone in the bar laughed...including big Davey

"Bloody daft bugger." Says Tucker reverting back to character...
"Yer looney...they'll come an' take yer away.."

Peter was a bit of a wide boy, who never missed a trick.
If there was owt to be had....he'd have it.

"Errrr!" Says peter casual like looking up from polishing his empty glasses...
he eyed Davey through a sparkling pint glass.
"As a matter of interest...given the chance, how much could yer eat?"
Big Davey gave out a laugh that shook all the glasses on the counter.

"Me!!" He says pointing to himself...he turned and picked up Tucker like
a little baby and sat him on the counter.
"I'd eat him with salt an' pepper!!"
Peter laughed...Tucker reddened.

"Funny buggar..." He said, climbing down and grumbled...
"Giv' ova arsing about."

Peter laughed again.
"Be serious will you..." He asked.
"How much could you really eat?"

"It all depends!!" Said Davey...stopping to think about it...
"Some days when Am not owa hungry, A'd eat one more tattie than a pig...
other days when Am clammin' with the hunger....A'd eat the bloody pig as
well!!"

"Naw...seriously," Peter asked again.

"*Serious..*" Answered Davey..."*Show me some proper grub, an' I'll show yer how to bloody-well eat.*"

Tucker blinked both eyes and pushed his nose into Davey's face.
"*Brag...brag...bloody...brag!!*" He told him....
"*Yer full of wind an'piss!!*"

"*Shurrup, short-arse...or I'll eat yer!!*" ...Davey joked, and bit Tucker on the end of the nose.

"*Ouch!!!*"...Yelled Tucker jumping up-right..."*Now yer for it.*"..says he pulling back a clenched fist.

Davey stuck out his chin.

"*I'll show yer!!*"...Tucker threatened as he took a swing at Daveys' big chin.

The punch didn't arrive. Davey caught it easily and held onto Tuckers hand.

"*Tucker...*" He said, "*Divint gan daft...Am only kiddin' man.*"

But Tucker's anger was up....he jerked free.

"*You...you...you..*" he repeated..frustrated and tried to think of something to get back at the big-fella.

"*Ha!!*" Tucker laughed at the wicked plan hatching in his duck-egg of a head....
"*So!!..yer think yer can eat big-fella...*" Before Davey could answer, he cut in... "*Let's hev a little wager...say ten quid.*"

"*Twenty!!*" Says Davey inspired.

"*Fifty!!*" Tucker shouts without thinking.

"*now, now lads.*" Peter butted in....
"*Had yer horses...divvint get carried away!!*"

Finally Tucker nodded...
"Right then, say twenty-five quid, I'll bet yer....me mate will out-eat yer!!"

"It's a deal." Says Davey, spitting in the palm of his hand.
Tucker did likewise....they shook hands.

Peter smiled to himself, he looked over the moon....
"Where an' when?"... he asked...
"How about right here, I'll judge an' supply all the grub?"

"Why..?" Tucker asked.

"Advertising...Free publicity, it'll empty all the bars on the Road, an' A'll make a killing."
"Sounds fine to me." Tucker said, nodding his head...
"But I want proper grub.." he finished.

"Such as...?" Peter asked............*"Can I make a suggestion?"*

"Gan on." Says Tucker.

.............*"Pies!!"* Says Peter.

"Meat?" Asked Davey.

"Oh Aye....the best steak an' kidney money can buy." Peter finished.

"Champion." Said Tucker and laughed....
"Just as long as they ain't pork, Henry don't eat pork!!"

"Don't give the tiniest shit what we eat so long as it's meat." Davey grunted.......
"Anyway, who the fuck's 'Enry?"

....

Davey, gaped up at the enormous hand painted sign, taped against the inside of Peters' window. It proclaimed.................

****

BIG PIE EATIN' CONTEST

And in letters almost as large…

HERE – SAT'DA NIGHT 8.00PM

Eagerly, Davey read the rest of it……

"The Reigning Champion"

DAVEY "THE PIG" … weight 19 st

- VS –

"The Leading Contender"

HENRY "THE HOG" … weight 25 st

****

A roar went up from the mob waiting inside, as Davey entered.

The bar was crammed. More than 200 men stood packed tight together, forming a semi-circle around the bar counter.

Davey felt a hand on his shoulder…

"Yer look in great shape champ." Said Peter.

"Are yee takin' the piss!!" Asked Davey.

"How'd yer feel?" Peter replied.

"Bloody –well great!!" ……Peter nudged Davey and gave him a wink…. *"Got some inside info on this Fella Henry. They reckon he's not feeling owa cleva… off his grub. My money's on you kid."*

214

Davey grinned.

Peter was wearing a black an' white stripped top-hat....a Newcastle United top and Bermuda shorts.

"What a night, what a bloody great night." Peter yelled over the din...
"Yer ever see such a crowd-eh!! Davey lad..."

Davey shook his head and reached for his beer, he downed it in one go.

"There's been more than five-hundred quid bet already...........Want another pint mate?"

"Don't mind if I do, helps get the owld taste buds gannin'."

A roar went up as Tucker suddenly appeared at the back of the Bar, he was wearing a tee-shirt, a City-Baths towel hung around his narrow shoulders.

"Cannit see the other fella." Peter said, stretching his neck.

Davey ignored the commotion, he leaned casually on the bar, like a gunfighter in a wild west saloon.
Everyone stopped talking....a voice cried, *"BLOODY HELL!!!"*

"Davey, is that right, yer can eat one tattie more than a pig!!" Peter asked.....

Davey turned his head, *"Yer callin' me a liar?"*

"Naw.." Says Peter.... *"It's just now's yer chance to prove it!!"*

"Meet Henry.." Said Tucker... *"Say hello to Davey...Henry."*

The huge mouth gaped open, saliva drooled through twisted tusk-like teeth.

"Gru...u...nt!!" Snorted Henry....The Vietnamese Pot-Bellied Pig.

215

"A fiver on der pig." Big Maloney yelled from the back.

Big Maloney and Little Maloney shouldered their way into the room, everyone stood quietly watching them as they pushed and shoved their way towards the front.

Big Mal and Little Mal were identical twins, the same in everyway, except that Big Mal had been born first. Large muscular men with jet black hair, they were a couple of hard-cases, who worked as bouncers over the town.

"We're nearly ready to start." Peter announced, looking at the clock high on the wall.

"Time limit...one-hour. The one who eats the most is the winner...Pies at the ready."

Bella the Bar-Maid, stood at the ready, a large steak 'n' kidney pie in each hand. Peter hollered....

"Start....eeee...eatin'....NOW!!"

Henry immediately swallowed his first pie whole.

Davey began more slowly and finished his pie in three bites and a swallow.

Money began appearing all over the room.

A fight almost started in the corner...the noise was tremendous.

Betting continued heavy.

Henry justified the favoured odds by finishing the second pie a full minute before Davey.

"Five more on der pig." Shouted Little Mal.

Davey pacing himself, settled into a gulping rhythm.

"Look it that mouth in motion...." Pop-eyed Reilly yelled.....

"I've gorra winner me."

The sixth pie had the fastest time of all.

Henry was obviously enjoying himself, showing no signs of slowing up and Davey was well into his stride.

..................................The betting grew heavier.

The odds on Henry went down and Lennie the Lever over in the corner was giving three to one on.

"Dat pig's a winner." Someone shouted.

"He effin' better be." Big Mals voice warned....." **or else**!!"

But suddenly Davey seemed stronger than ever...having gained a second wind.

The odds on Henry suddenly dipped when out of the blue he stopped eating...Davey made up ground.
Henry, cross-eyed stared at his pie.
Tucker gently put his hands on Henrys' bulging stomach...Henrys' eyes rolled.

"Yer gorra do it." Begged Tucker...... *"C'mon..c'mon."*
Henry snorted, broke wind then swallowed his pie.

The crowd groaned...Davey had faltered, he could only stare at his half eaten pie.
"Finish it yer useless shit." Pop-eye yelled.
Davey turned to face him... *"Shur-rup..."* He said... *"A'm pacing me'sel!!"*

But it was obvious to the crowd that Davey was tiring..but so was Henry.

After the twelfth pie, Little Geordie Willis began taking bets that neither would be able to finish the fourteenth.

Awaiting the Thirteenth pie, Tucker massaged Henry's stomach,...and told him... *"Yer got him worried Hen', yes yer have."*
Henry snorted but Davey was oblivious to the fact and gulped his pie steady, eyes closed.

As Bella lay down the 15th pie...The tension was tremendous.
Everyone was yelling, jumping up and down, clapping their hands in wild rhythm.

Henry was dreadfully weak, hardly able to stand.
Tucker...tears in his eyes, stood proudly beside him...his hands clenched, muscles white.
It was obvious to everyone that Henry was going on heart alone.

"Kick that effin' pig into gear.." Little Mal roared...*"Git him gannin'!!"*

Davey strained, he held his pie like a hundred weight bag of coal.

Lenny the Lever yelled...*"Five – to – one on for the big fella."*

Davey belched and retched...he tried a feeble smile, that didn't come off. It was inevitable...What went down was almost ready to come back up.

No one took the bet!!

Davey was almost done for.
But Henry was even in worse shape. His eyes were closed...he could barely nibble the pie before him.
Henry licked his lips...Wearily he tried to lie down.

Davey dug deep and drove himself to one more superhuman effort.
He lifted the pie slowly...raising it to eye level.
A lone voice urged him on...*"Gan'on, gan'on!!"*
But the weight was too much, Davey wobbled and swayed..an' then he dropped it... **"SPLAT!!!** "....................a steak an' kidney volcano erupted on the counter.

"I'm knackered..." Davey admitted and stretched out full length on the floor like a beached whale.

"We gorr' im beat." Yelled Big Mal.....
"Eat yer rotten swine, bloody-well eat!!" He screamed at Henry.

Tucker looked lovingly down at his pig.
"Yer done great." He whispered....
"Yer me best mate, yes yer are."
                              Henry snorted back....

Game to the end, Henry studied the pie. His snout crawled over the pie-crust, sniffing as it went.
His mouth lolled open the bubbles of saliva dribbled out.

With a wobble and a grunt...Henry rolled over onto his back...trotters in the air.

Peter announced, looking at the clock high on the wall...
"The match is a draw!!"

Although disappointed, the crowd buzzed softly in nothing but admiration for the fallen heroes.

"It was a great fight." Pop-eye Reilly said proudly.

"Oh aye!!, fair an' square." Lenny the Lever agreed

"What a bloody night, what a great bloody night." Peter almost sung.

Everyone was happy except....Little Mal, he sniggered, lips curled up.
"That pig of yours, he's got no effin' guts."

Tucker straightened....*"Yer had better take that back."* He wailed....
"He's nearly bloody killed his sel'."

"Eff – Off!!" Big Mal answered for his twin.
Then he did the unforgivable...he kicked the pig.

With a cry, Tucker ran at him.
Stepping aside big Mal drove a huge flat hand into Tucker's chest, sending him flying backwards against the bar counter, he hit it with a sickening thud, the wind knocked out of him....Slowly he sank to his knees helpless.

A hush fell over the bar...then Davey was on his feet, he yelled....
"That pig's got more bottle than any bugga in Byker!!"

With that..."**SMACK**!!!!", A giant right fist crashed on the side of Big Mal's jaw.

Big Mal half pivoted and crumpled to the floor.

"Hey!!", Cried Little Mal.…*"No buggar does that to me bro…th…"*
He didn't finish the sentence.…"**SMACK**!!!"
Little Mal lay next to his brother.

Davey lifted tucker to his feet.
"Yer OK mate?"…..…Tucker didn't hear, he'd dropped to his knees.

The bar stayed silent.…
So sad was the scene that it brought a tear to Pop-eye Reillys glass-eye.

Cradling Henry's head in his arms, Tucker cried like a baby.

Davey's face went a greenish white.…
He ran for the bog.…Where he brought up half his guts.

◘   Poor owld Henry had died of natural causes, which probably saved the Maloney twin's bacon.

◘   The funeral was held at Tucker's allotment, everybody in Byker was there. They buried owld Henry deep in Tucker's leek trench.

Over-night, Tucker's leeks took on gigantic proportions.…

The Annual Leek show prize giving is held in Peter's bar.

Every year, without fail, Peter presents a grinning Tucker with the First Prize Trophy.…..…
Big Davey and little Tucker came into the bar five minutes to twelve.…
I glanced at my watch and gave it a shake, the second hand jerked and kicked back in motion.
Like I says, regular as clock work.…you can set your watch by them.

Man versus Beast...

In the Big Eat

THE END

OWA THE BRIDGE

By Mark James

"Owa The Bridge."

Me mate Tommy is a bit of a living legend.
Years ago, he actually jumped off The Tyne Bridge and lived to tell the
tale.

Nahh!!... I tell a lie, he never did tell the tale, to this very day, the tale had
never been told.
So when right out of the blue he says,
"Remember the time I went an' hoyed me'sel owa The Bridge??"
"Why-aye." I nodded agreeing.
He went on to say, "See yer in The Raby tonight...sharpish an' I'll tell yer
the true tale."
I couldn't believe me ears.

Come opening time...I was first through the door.
The news had certainly spread fast....in no time at all, the place was
heaving.
I knew that it would cost us the price of a few pints, but I wasn't bothered,
it was cheap at the price.
I wasn't daft?...I knew for a fact that Tommy was using me.
He needed to, to tell the tale.

The crowd were getting restless – Tommy was late.
"Geordie!!...there's ganna be a bit of bother here!" Bella the buxom barmaid
warned.
Geordie? That's not me real name by the way, but that's what they called
us.
Why?...God only knows.
Just when I starts to get these naggin' doubts that he wasn't going to turn
up...the Bar door burst open and I breathe a sigh of relief as Tommy makes
his big entrance.

Some Joker whistled High Noon as Tommy swaggered over to us.
"Hi-ya Kidda!!" Tommy drawled, shaking my hand with one hand and
slapping me hard on the back with the other.
It made a lovely gesture.
Tommy leaned, propping himself up on the bar...elbow on the counter.
A pint of Best Scotch in his hand, I stood right next to him and thought

to meself, my God, he's the double of Stan Laurel...!!

I wonder if I looked like Oliver Hardy?

The place went quiet before I realized that we were standing there like a couple of actors on Centre Stage.

I could hear the Laurel and Hardy Theme tune in me head.

I'm thinking...This is another fine mess he's got us into – It certainly is!!

Tommy took a swig of beer and wiped the froth from his mouth with his coat sleeve.

"Aaaahhh....Pure Nectar." He gasped.

"Sorry'am late." He Joked,

"Aa had me watch on upside down!"

The strange thing is I wondered how I'd never noticed it before –

He didn't just look like Stan Laurel, he also spoke like him...in that slow story telling voice of his.

Tommy always had short arms and deep pockets, so it was a pleasant surprise to see his hand go in.

For a moment of madness I thought he was going to get the drinks in... but I was proved wrong.

He pulled out a crumpled newspaper cutting, yellowed with age.

"Hev a good look at that Geordie me owld mate!!"

He said and made a big show of spreading it out on the counter like a treasure map.

"Made the front page." He stated...loud and proud.

The bar went quiet.

You couldn't hear a swear word...a glass clink....or even the slurp of beer.

They'd all waited years to hear this.

Tommy wasn't going to disappoint them.

He spun around on his heels and took a little bow.

Then he recited the headline that he knew and loved so well....

"Byker Man Falls from Tyne Bridge"

Then he laughed...just like he did at one of his own jokes.

Tommy was a born comedian, everyone agreed that he should have went on stage.

"Fell!!!....Me Arse!!" Tommy sniggered.

"Funny, how they never ever say jumped." Tommy took a swig of beer, then paused to ponder.

I could almost see a thought bubble popping out of his head.

"It was 1959." He stated loud and clear.

"Twenty years of age I was...and just come out of the Daft an' Barmy, two bloody years National Service!!...

...What a waste. It felt just like getting outa jail."

It was hard not to laugh, he was hardly ever out the Army...Clink.

"Me!!" said Tommy pointing to himself...

"Aa couldn't wait to make up for lost time, well you know what 'am like." He said looking at me.

"Never had nowt in me life. Dragged up I was."

"Aye..." I had to agreed"...but weren't we all Tommy Lad, weren't we all?" I continued.."And we expected nowt..it's just the way it was then, we knew no other."

And for once in his life Tommy agreed.

"Exactly!!" he yelled. Thumping a clenched fist on the bar counter.

"But the Army changed all of that.... Getting' outa Byka and seein' the world, made me want a hell of a lot more outa' life." He Finished.

"Only natural...I suppose." I agreed..."It's called growing up."

"Yer can say that again!!" Tommy said nodding his head.

"Went in the Army a Mouse...would settle for a little bit of cheese...Came out a hungry Lion wantin' bloody-red-meat!!" He retorted.

"Yer wanted meat?" I asked.

Tommy answered.." Naw Geordie man, it's just a figure of speech. Aa wanted more than that. I wanted a life."

He repeated whistfully..Tommy stated..."***Wanted a bloody Life!!***"

"Life's what yer make it." I told him...

"Yer gotta make good things happen..they don't happen themselves?"

Tommy smiled, he really was full of himself now as the drink kicked in.

"Now yer talkin'...that's what I'm trying to say. I took the bloody Bull by the effin' horns!!"

He said and demonstrated by gripping the beer pump handles.

Some joker started to, "Mooo..." Cow like.

....

That was Tommy all over, he'd been around the World and his journey hadn't even started.

"Just imagine.." Tommy continued, looking at his freshly pulled pint....
"Me in me prime..." Tommy pumped out his chest and strutted on the spot.
"Fit as a lop, strong as an Ox and as daft as a bloody brush...Aa was ready to take on the bloody whole world....but little did I know t'was the World who would take on me!!".

He was really talking to an audience now, they hung on his every word.
"Thought I was Jack the Lad, but ended up – Tommy owa The Bridge.... When I was a kid I worked me Bollocks off for nowt and now here I was for the first time in me life with a proper job with real money."
"'Ere, and how do yer mean..." Bella asked..
"Real money?...what other kind is there?" ...She had little value for money.
"What 'am trying to say...I was a man doin' a man's job." Tommy preached and lifted his arms...fingers outstretched...like Jesus giving a sermon.
"For the first time in me life I had money...real money in me poke."
Bella gave him a look that said she was none the wiser...she'd never been hard up.

"The World was me Oyster." Said Tommy.
He reached out with clutching fingers and grabbed hold of something big and round.
I couldn't say for certain, but I think he had a hold of the World...
Bella sang.."He's got The Whole World in his hands..." That got a laugh.
Tommy stood and proud and regal....like the King of The World....as Bella finished the song, everyone whistled, cheered and clapped...it all seemed part of the act.

Tommy was now in Seventh Heaven!!...He threw Bella a kiss...that missed by a mile.

Tommy took a long swig of his beer, then burped.
His eye's sparkled now as they did when he talked about money and what it can buy...as only those who knew real poverty could.
"Aa'll tell yer this for nowt!!" Tommy said looking at me.
"Remember pressin' our nose flat against the shop window and wishin' our lives away?" He finished.

- And I can remember how I only wished for a gobstopper while, Tommy wanted the Moon –

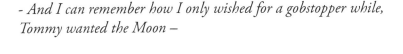

Tommy continued....
"There was ganna be nay more dead men's clothes for me, I can tell yer."

And that dusty-foisty smell from The Panshop came back to me and the shame of
having to take me Fatha's best suit in.
Running home with a couple of Bob to feed the Family and face the fear in me motha's
face and the panic in her voice as she sent me running like Hell down our back lane to
redeem it.
I gripped that half-crown so tight that even now I can still imagine a sweaty red circle
baring The Kings head indented in the palm of me hand.

....

"Funny you should say that?" I told Tommy...
"When I come to think of it you always used to stink of moth-balls!!"
Tommy took the huff and went on the defence stating....
...."Huh!! Kidda, you needn't talk, all your good gear came off yer Uncle Joe' rag-an-bone cart!!"
"It's true.." I replied.."I can't argue with that....but then again, it isn't me that's telling the tale....is it!!"

Tommy ignored that and went back to spending yesterday's money.
"With coming out'a the Army, I was in limbo, everything had changed...it was all happenin'...Rock 'n' Roll, mini skirts, an' those sexy stiletto heels... Me, I looked an' felt like I didn't belong. It was as if life had passed me by and I was gonna be an' Owld man before me time."
"Aye Tommy." I nodded me head in agreement, I knew the feeling.
Our Generation had missed out on being Teenagers.
One day you were a Kid at School...and the next day you were a working man.

"Every Bugga gets owld!!" mocked Bella..."Who did yer think you were, ...Peter – Bloody – Pan!!"

Tommy laughed.."Oh aye, that was me alright. I wanted to never get Wed...never have kids and live happily ever after...In Never-Never Land.. Just like Peter Pan."

A murmer of discontentment ran through the Bar.
I caught the drift.
It seemed, they were all old men well before their time and lived on the never-never.

Tommy asked Bella for a bag of crisps.
She handed them over, telling him politely to, "Stick'em up your arse!!"
Tommy looked at me, then smacked his lips and stared lovingly at his empty glass.
"Now were was Aa?" He yelled.
"Bloody Never-Never Land!!" Came the yell from the crowd.
"Aye." Mocked Bella..."I've noticed yer Never-Never-Ever get yer turn in?"
It was water off a ducks back for Tommy.
He took a sup of his beer and smacked his lips...and burped.

"Back then."...he started..."Fashion was all the rage....so I had to move with the times...I became a dedicated follower of fashion."
"Aye, I can just see you in a mini skirt and sexy stiletto heels." I laughed.
Tommy replied quickly, "So Aa 'gans an' buys a couple of them flashy made to measure Italian suits."

A sigh of pure happiness went around the bar as middle aged men remembered their flashy made to measure Italian suits...Tony Curtis hair-cuts and their long lost youth.
And as if rehearsed, they sang as one-

"Wide Shouldered Short jacket- Tight Trousers..."

Tommy as ever came in right on cue...
"An if i say so me-self, I looked bloody well great!!...Aa gans the whole hog and gets a boot-lace-tie and a couple of pairs of handmade Italian shoes."
"Them little lightweight things?" ..I asked..."With pointed toes, they fit yer like a glove."

228

"Aye, that's 'em." Says Tommy nodding his head...."Yer didn't Knaa yer had the bugga's on."

He emphasised this by dancing a little jig on his toes.

"Aa spent like a millionaire." He bragged.

Bella shot him down..."Put a beggar on a horse-back an' he'll ride to Hell."

"Yer not wrong." Tommy replied to Bella....

"Me!!...I always thought money was the answer to all me prayers, I spent it just for the sake of spending....gans an' gets me'sel a few luxuries."

"Such as?"..I asked.

Tommy looked embarrassed, he scratched the stubble on his chin before answering..."Now Geordie pal...don't laugh."

I said I wouldn't, but to tell the truth....I lied.

"Now yer promised not to laugh." Tommy repeated more to himself than to anyone else....

"Well..." He started then hesitated..."Now I know this sounds a bit daft, but I always did fancy one of them gold medallions hangin' around me neck." I looked at Bella and Bella looked at me....

We both looked at Tommys' skinny neck and his billiard ball Adam's Apple. – Bella was hysterical...it took a double Brandy to calm her down. All I said was, *"Look-up, here comes Mr Medallion Man."* Just as Tommy came strutting out the bog – I think that set her off.

"Divin't look at 'im!!" I whispered to her as Tommy arrived on the scene.

The first words Bella spoke when she'd got her breath back were aimed at Tommy – "Bloody poser!!"...He took it as a compliment, rolling his shoulders he stuck out his boney chest.

"Y'knaa." Tommy grinned...

"Aa' suppose I am Byka's answer to Elvis Presley?"

"Aye!" says Bella.. "Up yer own arse an' all shook up."

Tommy started to shake his hips, curled up his lip and gave her his best Elvis Presley look.

"Anyway, I gans and gets this great big solid gold medallion..."..he started again. .. "...There was this owld fella on it...he was plodgin' through water with a kid on his back."

"That would be St Christopher, the Patron Saint of Travellers." I stated.

"Aye...that's the fella, St what's-ees-name?....wore me medallion round me neck with me shirt open."

Bella started giggling again when he said, "As big as a bin lid it was."

Making a huge circle with his hands.

That was when she started laughing again and ran to the ladies.... Bella could hold her drink but not her pee....I doubted if she made it.

....

Tommy's glass was empty now so I poured half mine into his, to keep the tight fisted owld bugger going.

"Went the whole hog and bought a snake ring from the panshop. Bloody marvellous it was, 22carat gold with little red ruby eyes."

Tommy smiled dreamily at the wonder of it all, then his eyes lit up. He nudged me in the side...

"Remember me watch?...Stainless steel.. Iimitation Rolex.. I brought it back from Hong Kong."

"Remember it..." I said...

"Once seen never forgotten...I thought you'd got it off King bloody Kong man!!"

Tommy laughed... "You were only jealous."

"Aye mebees I was, I'd never had a watch." I replied.

"What a time piece..." Tommy bragged... "Shockproof, waterproof, illuminous dial..."

Tommy glanced at the bar mirror...a stranger looked back and for a moment he looked sad.

His eye's glazed over and he looked at the picture he had of himself in his head.

"Whey Geordie man, yer should have seen us back them." He said dreamily. I reminded him..."I did!!"

And cringed at the memory...."Yer only looked bloody well great."....I lied.

Tommy smiled at that..." Aaa did mate."

He continued "Aye, didn't I just...an yer didn't look too bad yersel' Geordie mate!!"....I had to laugh.

"There's nowt wrong with blowin' yer own trumpet Kidda!!"...

Tommy boasted, and he should know...after all, he was a one man band.

....

The trouble with Tommy, he lived in his own little fantasy world...he'd never grew up and never would.

Me I reckon it all began the very first time he'd entered the local Picture

230

hall...I know, because I was with him.

Tommy didn't just look at the Film's, he lived them.

He became the Hero...the Star of every Picture-show....Always leaving the Hall with Stars in his eye's.

Tommy spent half his childhood shouting "SHAZZAM!!!", up at the sky and expecting a bolt of lightning to strike and change him into "Captain Marvel". The other half of his childhood was spent jumping off backyard walls and trying to fly.

....

Tommy's eye's sparkled...they were watery and bloodshot but the stars were still there.

"Can yer imagine...Aa looked just like a Film Star!!" said Tommy into his empty glass.

"Aye.." says Bella... "Charlie Chaplin!!"

Tommy turned a deaf-ear....."Yer should have seen us commin'."

"Seen yer commin!!" Mocked Bella..."Couldn't bloody-well miss you.... Yer had more edge than a broken piss-pot!!"

Tommy reflected..."It's funny you should say that, she definitely saw me coming alright."

When Tommy said She, a murmmer of excitement went through the bar.

This was gonna be better than *"The News of The World."*

Again Tommy looked at his empty glass...this time I was only to happy to get them in.

"Met her in The Bigg Market...Saturday Night it was."

Tommy said before taking a sup and smacking his lips...."Me I was half pissed at the time and didn't give a shit."

Tommy glanced at Bella...She was no oil painting.

"An' if her face was her fortune...she'd have died of hunger."

Bella gave him a dirty look and spat.."Huh!!...Elvis Presley me arse." As she went out to the back of the bar she muttered over her shoulder....."More like Bobby bloody Thompson....Yer shower of shit!!".

Tommy continued in that slow sing-song voice of his, "Just imagine..." he said and gave a wolf whistle and with his hands formed an hour-glass

231

figure in mid air.

He left nothing to the imagination...

"Oh aye, she was all woman...but she drunk and swore like a man!!...

....Me I couldn't keep me eyes off her...I was what was the word?"

"Lunatic comes to mind." Said Bella arriving back on the scene.

Scratching his head, deep in thought, Tommy chirped...."Infatuated, that's the word!!...She had something about her that turns yer on... Er what-yer-calls-it again?"

Searching his brain, he was running out of meaningful words.

"Personality..?" I offered.

"Aye...Geordie, I suppose so...well that and greet big tits!!" Tommy added.

Bella almost blushed, I'd never seen that before.

"It's a bloody good job I'm an effin' lady." She shouted at Tommy and threw him a dirty look.

It was water off a ducks back.

"Aye, like I says, her face was nowt to look at, but the more I drank, the better she looked. Come closing time, I was as pissed as a fart...and she looked bloody-well gorgeous...and anyway, yer don't look at the mantle-piece when yer poking the fire!!" He finished.

....

Tommy took a long hard swig of his pint and burped.

"She called hersel' Rosie...couldn't say for sure if that was her real name... She came from owa Gateshead an' she wasn't called *The Local Bike*" for nowt and me...I was dying for me leg-owa and Rosie she took me for a ride." Somebody at the back started singing....

"Rosie Oh... Rosie, I'd like to paint your face up in the sky..."

Everyone in the bar joined in, as Tommy pretended to play a one man band. "Although I've just met you...I can't quite forget you...I'd like to paint your face eternally...Dee..Dee..Dee..Dee..Dee – Born..Born!!"

Tommy finished with a roll on the drum.

He now paused for effect and closed his eye's...

"Next morning...I opened me eye's." And that's what he did, rolling them skyward.

"And yer Knaa, for a minute there, I thought I was paralysed."

"How do yer mean...paralysed?" I asked.

"I couldn't bloody move...could I...Rosies powerful legs were wrapped around me thighs in a vice like grip, stoppin' the blood flowing through me veins...I could feel pins and needles in me toes....

...A mighty arm had me in a powerful head-lock...and me nose was as flat as a pancake against a coconut bicep..." Tommy explained.

"Aa' nearly shit me-sel'....I lay face to face with a grinning skull an' cross-bone tattoo. I squinted me eye's and some words came into focus...They Read....

"DEATH BEFORE DISHONOUR"

.....An' I'm thinking to meself, does that mean me...Jesus, I'm too young to die!!"

A murmur went through the bar and I caught the drift.

They were all in agreement.... *"What a lovely way to go."*

Tommy looked at his glass, licked his lips and nodded...it was as good as a wink...He continued with relish...

"Her mouth was wide open, she was snorin' like a pig. Outa' the corner of me eye I could see her false teeth grinnin' at me from a pint glass.

Me medallion lay on the pillow and the chain wasn't around my neck...it was around hers'.

And I got to thinking...it's right what me owld Granda' used to say about sex...once you've had it, you don't bloody want it!!...

...she opened her mouth as big as Tynemouth."....

"Wass-is-yer-name?" She groaned without even bothering to open her pools of black mascara eye's.

"Who me??" I croaked.

"Who the 'effin' else!!" She snarled..

"T-T-Tommy..." I stuttered..."And I hadn't stuttered since I was a little bairn."

"Pleased ter meet yer...Me bonny lad." She says all sarcastic like...then she opens a Brown, Blood-shot eye.

"An' before I even had a chance to ask her for me medallion back she opens the other eye. ...And I blinked cause I couldn't believe me own eye's...Jesus, it was blue."...

"Aa lay there pondering the mystery of life and death...nowt made any sense, nowt at all....She must have heard what I was thinking cause she laughs an empty hollow laugh with no joy in it at all." Tommy reminisced. "Then she pops in her false teeth and gives me a false smile, before tellin' me the good news."

"Oh by the way bonny lad, congratulations!!" She stated.

"Eh??....What for??..I asked."

"Don't yer remember bonny lad...then I suppose I'll hev' to remind yer then"... and she flashed me snake-ring..it was on her bloody engagement finger!!"

"We're engaged to be married...You're gonna try and make an honest woman *outta me."* She explained.

"Is Aa??....I croaked."

"Why aye!!" She mocked and stuck out her tongue...

...*"The happy day takes place on the 7th of June...Seventh time lucky...Eh??"*

Tommy paused..." Me I was a little bit worried like 'cos I'd already booked up to gan to Butlins with me mates – the Second week in June....

....The funny thing is I honestly thought it was all a bad dream and I'd wake up and forget all about it, like yer usually do."

...He continued, "....But then I hears a slow deep Female voice that seemed to come from a long way off."

The voice demanded...*"Will yer jump up an' make us a nice cuppa tea pet.... Milk an' Two Shugga's...Ta!!"*

"When I'm kicked outa the bed...Bollock naked!!....I knew for a fact it wasn't a dream." Tommy concluded.

"Don't go away..." Says Tommy... "I'm just away for a piss."

The bar erupted, there was a mad stampede for the bogs...everyone was bursting for a piss.

....

Bella sprung into action, pulling pints at the double.

The drinks lay in line the length of the bar counter.

Heavy boots shuffled on saw-dust, over-flowing glasses clinked and splashed down on hardwood tables.

Stools and Chairs grated...arses parked...beer bellies wobbled.

Shipyard workers and Miners coughed and hacked, spitting to clear their lungs....Then "HUSH!!"....then silence.

Tommy took centre stage a pint in hand.

"Then what happened?"...I asked..."Gan on tell us!!"

Tommy's eye's looked vacant as he turned to me for help..
"Geordie...where was Aa?" He asked.
"Yer back in the bed!!" a lone voice yelled from the back.
Every head in the bar turned to the direction of the voice and yelled as one..."Eff-Off!!"......Then they turned back to Tommy...
and yelled even louder...."Yer run like Bloody Hell!!"
"Sorry..." said Tommy...."Me mind was runnin down Gatesheed High Street...but me body was weak...it jumped back into the bed."

He smiled dreamily and his eye's glazed over and he took a long adams-apple bobbling swig of his pint...Time travel was pretty thirty work!!

"We lived on nowt but Love...Newcastle Brown Ale an' Fish 'n' Chips."
He told his pint of beer.
"Love..." I Laughed...and gave him a look that said...pull the other leg.
"Aye Love...!!" Tommy said, holding his hand to his heart and pretending to be hurt..." She made me feel a bit special."
"Yer takin' the piss...she's old enough to be yer granny!!" I said.
"Yer know what they say?" Tommy replied.
"What do they say?" I answered.
"Geordie Man....Love is blind." He responded with feeling.
"Bloody blind drunk.." Mocked Bella.
Tommy admitted..." Well mebee's it was a funny kind of love....but you know me, I've always been infatuated by older women....It was a bit like that film an, what-cher-yer – call-it?"

"Oh aye...Beauty and the Beast!!" I joked.
"Naw man...Samson an' Delilah." He said.

Everybody laughed at the thought of Tommy killing a Lion with his bare hands and Heidi Lamar giving him a short back and sides.
"Just like Samson, I was a slave to love....There was no escape and I'm not sure that I wanted to either...She was the spider and I was the fly."
"Black widow!!....Tommy eh..!" Someone Heckled.
"Naw Geordie...she was white as a ghost an covered in freckles...but her hair was as black as coal an' hung down her back, right to the cheeks of her bum...mind, she had a lovely bum." ....He continued..
"In me heart of hearts, I knew it wouldn't last...Aa was a glutton for punishment. These days, I'd have been called a sex slave...it wasn't me

screwin' her, it was her screwin' me."

A murmur went through the bar and I caught the drift.

It seemed that they all would die for the chance to become a sex-slave and live a life of Riley on love, broon-ale an' Fish 'n' Chips wi' batter on!!

"Love!!" Yelled Bella...."More like lust!!"

And she should know, she used to be on the batter...

> *Hips swaying...half closed eyes....glistening red mouth...*
> *....Love for sale...emptied of feeling, desire and need.*
> *Like a sleep-walker who never knew day....*
> *"Looking for business Dear?" ....Sexy smile.*
> *"Short time?...All nighter whatever yer fancy – It's all in the game..."*

"Yer a dirty Owld Bugga." Bella seemed to say more to herself than Tommy. She leans over the counter and looks at Tommy with squinted eye's and a sexy smile...and she says with passion..."Gizz-a-Kiss!!"

Tommy took a step back and took a long hard look at Bellas' Crimson pouting lips.

"Naw thanks.." He said..."I'd rather pull a rabbit outa me arse!!"

Owld Frankie who'd always lusted after Bella nearly swallowed his false teeth.

"That ain't no way to talk to a Lady." He said to Tommy.

Everybody laughed...including Bella who laughed 'til she cried.

....

Tommy was on a high now...there was no stopping him...he kissed Bella's hand and ducked as the other hand formed a fist that went sailing over his head.

Tommy was given a round of applause as he did a little jig of joy.

"This night..." Tommy began...lifting a hand to the hushed crowd...

"We'd been owa the Toon...me an' Her."

He then stopped and coughed and looked down at his empty glass.

....

Tommy once more took centre stage.

In Tommy's mind, he was on at The Grand...

.......the spotlight was on him, he was the star of the show.

He held his captive audience in the palm of his hand and a pint of Best Scotch in the other.

Tommy pumped out his chest...his eyes lit up, he grinned from ear to ear...a lunatic grin.

"Now were was Aa?"...he spoke to the crowd.

"Owa the Toon!!" Every voice in the room yelled back....Tommy continued.

"We had a canny drink an' a bite to eat...missed the last bus we did!!"

"It was a lovely night...we strolled owa the Tyne Bridge. It was one of those magical nights...a full moon and a sky full of stars...their reflections danced on the oily water. It was very romantic like...It was one of those nights when daft people do daft things....and there was no bugga dafter than me!!" He finished.

"Yeah...I'll drink to that." Bella said.

Tommy ignored Bella and went on..." Rosie started singin' – *"By the light of the silvery moon"*...Now I know Rosie was no Doris Day but she could hold a tune. An' me all of a sudden as if by magic started to Dance....I couldn't help me-self...don't ask me why, cause me!!!...I used to hate dancing and I'd never danced in me bloody life.

....But like I say, it was one of them magical nights."

Tommy danced a little dance –

"If yer so happy...why did yer gan and jump off the bloody bridge." Owld Frankie asked.

"Had on a minute...I'll cross that bridge when I come to it!!" 'Tommy replied.

"Yer already on the bloody bridge." Bella reminded him....

...."Yer barmy bugga!!"

"What am trying to say...it was all an act.....it wasn't real.....nowt seemed real!!" Tommy explained....

"In me heart I wasn't really happy...was I."

"Then why were yer dancing?" Owld Frankie spoke like a prosecution Lawyer in front of the Judge and Jury.

It was a lovely night
We strolled owa the bridge
It was one of those magical nights...

Tommy smiled an ironic smile and shook his head before answering.
"Don't know....why does a hanged man dance at the end of a rope??...God only knows!! Anyway, half way owa the bridge, Rosie stops singing. She elbows me in the ribs an says all romantic like....
"Keep an' eye open Bonny Lad...'am bursting for a piss!!"
"I'll tell you something for nowt..." Tommy continued..."I couldn't believe me luck... 'cos I'd been waiting for the chance to make me escape and this seemed as good a time as any to tell her nicely –
"Tarah!! 'am away back home to me Ma's.. " ..an' run like bloody hell!!"
"Good thinking." I said agreeing with him.." Catch her with her knickers doon like!!"
"Aye Geordie that was me plan but I never got the chance." Tommy replied, shaking his head slowly.." Before I'd the time to even open me gob...she looks over her shoulder an' tells me right outa' the blue...
"Guess what???....A'm expectin'."
He went on..."An' she says just as casual as you'd say...I've gorra spot on me bum!!"
"Couldn't believe me lugs could I....bloody expectin'!!" ...Tommy stated, Reflecting, Tommy continued..."Expectin' What!!"
"A little bundle of joy." She says all schmoozy.
"A bundle of what."
"Am havin' a bairn!!" She yells... *"You daft shite."*

"And to prove her right I was daft enough to ask her.. *"Who's is it then??""*
"An' who's do you think it is??" She says all sarcastic like... *"It's yours me Bonny Ladd...."* She kept going..."*So...it looks like a shotgun Wedding...or in other words – I've got yer by the balls!!"*
"Then she laughed a wicked laugh and yanks her knickers down and flashes me her bum......An' do you know what a'm thinking...she's got the arse like an elephant!!"..Tommy said.
"Aye..." He went on...
..."Apart from that...'am wonderin' how me poor old Ma will take it... She'll kill me stone bloody dead....Me brain was boilin' in me head...nowt made any sense...nowt at all!!"

After a sup Tommy kept going...
"An' for a minute I think I'm dreamin' 'cos...Aa can see the moon down on the ground, it's fallen from the sky and I can hear heavy rain stottin' off the pavement an' I'm bone dry!!....but naw, its only Rosie squatting down with her arse stuck up in the air...peeing like a horse!!!....

239

TOMMY LEAPT UP ON TO THE BAR COUNTER. I THINK
HE WAS MEANT TO BE STANDING ON THE TYNE
BRIDGE...

....The sight was enough to bring a tear to a glass-eye."
Tommy shook his head and a look of disbelief crossed over his face...
"What I saw in her...I'll never know."

A cry of **"Sex, broon-ale and Fish 'n' Chips!!"**.. came from the crowd.

"Aye.." said Tommy...
"I can't argue with that!!....The situation was desperate...me head was
about to explode...an' a funny thing happened....from outa nowhere this
lovely music came into me head."
Tommy paused for effect...then looked up-a-height and a tear came to his
eye.
"An this wonderful voice starts singing!!" ... Tommy stopped to think and
banged a fist on the counter...
"'Am buggered if Aa can remember that bloody song....but it came from
a great musical."
"Singin' in the Rain!!" I guessed wrongly.
"Naw." Says Tommy..."Anyway it kept on goin' through me head."
"How's it gan...hum it!!" Bella suggested...she was ready to burst into song.
"Mmm-mm-mm...La, La..La-La-La-La.." He hummed and La'hd out of
tune. The silence that followed spoke volumes.

If Tommy had to sing for his supper...He'd starve.

"Anyway.." said Tommy un-deterred..
"That song makes everyone cry...an he gans to heaven in the end."
"Who does??" Bella was brave enough to ask.
"Him...the fella in the film, an' he ends up polishin' the stars at the end.."
Tommy looked Heavenwards...
"Can yer imagine..polishing the bloody stars...warra way to go!!" He said
with feeling, his eyes sparkled as he pretended to polish imaginary stars.

....

The spell was broken when Tommy sprang into action...
Before you could say Jackie Milburn...Tommy leapt up on the bar
counter. He certainly moved pretty quick and graceful for an owld fella
with arthritis and bandy legs.

There he stood in a Charlie Chaplin pose, leaning on an imaginary rail. I think he was meant to be standing on the Tyne Bridge.

"Git yer dirty feet off me clean counter!!" Yelled Bella..Flicking at Tommy's arse with her wash-rag.

But Tommy wasn't here..He was back in the sixties on that eventful night. The night that changed the direction of his life.

Standing on The Tyne Bridge, looking down at the murky waters of the Tyne It was rather moving...no-one laughed, because with a belly full of beer it wasn't hard to imagine.

The bar went quiet...you could almost hear the frothy bubbles bursting in your glass.

Everyone in the bar were polishing stars.

Tommy laughed and did a little jig of joy...took a swig of ale...before he continued:-

"Aa takes a long hard look owa the bridge an jokes...I've a good mind to hoy mesel' owa!!"

"Yer haven't got the bloody guts." Rosie mocked.

"An' yer know what...she was right an' all..." Tommy continued....

..."But it didn't take guts to take the easy way out...an' she yells....

"Gan on then...jump yer bloody coward."

"An' honestly...I still don't know why I did...I just did...they honestly didn't call me King of cowards for nowt."....

....."An even bigger mystery is why I gave her me watch...didn't want to break it I suppose, wasn't really sure if it was shockproof or even waterproof, but it was definitely illuminous....'cause I could see the time glowing in the dark. Spot on 12 o'clock midnight, the magical hour...could even hear it ticking away....ain't it funny how yer remember the little daft things, when you think they are yer last...." He paused a moment reflecting...

"I'll never forget me parting words either...***"Tarrah!!"***...I yells over me shoulder...See yer in Hell!!"

With that said, Tommy started running on the spot.

I think it was meant to be his suicide run.

"Will yer give owa man!!" Yelled Bella...pretending to be angry...

"Yer loony bugger, yer rattlin' me clean glasses."

She was really enjoying it now...Tommy and her would have made a great double act.

Tommy broke his stride and blinked both eye's and came back to reality again.

Bella glared up at him and joked.."Why don't you just go and hang yersel' and be done with it, a rope cost's nowt!!"

"Hung mesel' once...didn't work..." He responded.."Aa just ended up talking like Daffy Duck!!"

"Bloody lunatic.." Said Bella and told him..."That's your bloody trouble.... you never finish owt yer start!!"

"Funny you should say that, it's jogged me memory. That was the last thing she said before I jumped..."

Tommy's eye's glazed over in less than a heart beat...our time-traveller was back on the Bridge running with a high stepping stride, towards the hand rail. Tommy was here in body on The Raby pub counter, running on the spot...but his mind and spirit gave a running commentary from The Tyne Bridge.

"The last thing I heard.." Tommy said...mid stride...

"As I leaped owa The Bridge hand rail, was someone screaming blue bloody murder and I'd like to think it was her." ...as he finally jumped off the bridge – Sorry, The Raby Bar counter.

"Bloody good riddance!!" Bella yelled...and everyone cheered, whooped and whistled as he hit the floor with an.."Uummmpphh!!"

Then he took a deep breath and told us...

"To tell the honest truth, it wasn't her that screamed...it was me!!"

With that said Tommy swivelled on his heels to face the counter and empties his glass with a gulp.

"Sorry about me going over the top at bit Kidda!!" Tommy said turning to face me.

"It's just sometimes I get a bit carried away like....well it's not every day a man get's to bounce back from the dead!"

"Same again love?" Bella asked....and answered.."These are on me."

Giving him an adoring smile with no sarcasm in it at all. It seemed to me that she saw Tommy in a different light.

....

The mood in the bar changed and became more melancholy.

Tommy had struck a raw nerve...the drink and the mood began to loosen tongues. A murmer went through the room and I caught the drift.

It seemed that every man in the room – and it wasn't the drink talkin' – had at one time or another contemplated suicide.

It's an awful thing for a man to admit, but once said soon forgotten and it doesn't pay to dwell on the poor souls that had given up on life...long before life had given up on them.

Yer had to laugh, is it me or is it the drink or is everyone stone mad.
One minute they're up in the clouds, the next diggin' their own grave!!

When Sammy Johnson spoke a hush came over the bar...'cause Sammy hardly ever spoke, and when he did it was well worth listening.

"Did yer life flash before yer?" Sammy asked in a deep voice that seemed to come from the grave..." 'Cause they reckon it does!!" He finished.

Sammy knew what he was talking about...he'd been there before.

Sammy had fought in the war and lost many a good mate.

Wounded in action, he'd came close to death many a time.

"Whaddy'a mean...Who's they like?" Tommy answered Sammy, not sure how to take him.

"Aa suppose it's them that's lucky enough to live and tell the tale." Sammy replied sadly.

Tommy pondered before answering because he knew for a fact, Sammy was an old soldier, a hero...whereas he himself was nowt but a bloody lunatic!! To rise from the dead was the only thing they had in common.

"Aye," Replied Tommy..."Maybe it does for some, but me!!..I never had much of a bloody life!!"

"Even so..." Said Sammy pointing a finger.."I'll tell yer something' for nowt. No matter how miserable yer life seems at the time...don't it suddenly seem sweet when yer realise it's about to end."

Tommy laughed with relief..."Yer can say that again." He agreed...and walked over to Sammy and shook his hand....and for a minute, they were Brothers in Arms.

It was a wonderful gesture.

Tommy turned to face the crowd..."It's right what Sammy says."

He laughed at himself.."Can yer believe it, an' this is no word of a lie."

Tommy laughed even louder this time..."On me way down, I only went and changed me bloody mind!!"

"Ah!!! a bit late in the day for that...wasn't it!!.." I tells him...

"There's nowt yer could do was there!!"

"There might be, but there was only one thing I could do!!" Tommy said.

"An' that was shit yersel'!!" I shouted.

"Naw!!.." He responded..."I only gans an' tries to bloody well fly!!"

"Yer didn't did yer?" Bella queried.

"Aa certainly did.." Tommy answered in that slow Stan Laurel voice of his.

Once again I can hear De-de-de didely –De...The Laurel and Hardy theme tune
bouncing along merrily in my head.

"Geordie man, just imagine one of them Tom & Jerry cartoons.

Yer know the one I mean. That one when Tom runs off the edge of the cliff and he doesn't know it 'til he looks down and there's a delayed reaction... before he flaps his arms like wings and hovers in mid-air then drops like a stone...That was me." Tommy finished.

That really did make me think...wondering if he's Tom....doesn't that make me Jerry.

This worries me 'cause I'm stuck with the Tom & Jerry theme tune... bouncing along merrily in my head.

The Bar is in uproar...They'd all seen and had never forgotten that particular Episode of Tom & Jerry.

Bella asked Tommy.."Did yer scream?"...

and she demonstrated, **"*Aaaarrrrggghhh!!!....*** like they do in the Pictures?"

"Bugger the pictures." Tommy replied....

"Anyway, I didn't have time to scream...did I!!"

"An' how's that then??" Bella asked.

"Simple." Says Tommy, "Aa was busy doing what any true Atheist would do, when he thinks he's on his way out."

"An' what's that then??" Bella asked puzzled.

Tommy and Sammy both laughed as if they had shared the same joke and smiled a knowing smile...it was if they could read each others mind.

"We only starts saying our bloody prayers!!" They both said.

All this dying and coming back from the dead almost made me want to believe in God.

From out of nowhere an old familiar voice came in...

"How did yer hit the water?" Owld Frankie asked.

"An' how do yer think," Tommy blurted sarcastically, "With a great big bloody splash!!"

Frankie replied.." Naw man, how did yer enter the water, head or feet first?" Owld Frankie read a lot of detective novels and had become a bit of a stickler for the facts....Nothing but the facts.

So Tommy humoured him..."Feet." He said....

"Aye..definately feet first!!"

"Did it hurt much?" Bella queried....then answered herself.."It must have done!!"

Tommy shook his head...

..."Naw, not really, well not at first anyway...Felt nowt at all, I was numb all over. Didn't know where I was, in fact, I thought I was dead....an' I'm looking down and I can see me own funeral....an' the funny thing is me Fatha was there an' the wicked owld bugga was laughing his head off. Everybody was happy, they were having a great time...an' our owld lady, she was dancin' a jig.

An' I'm lying in me coffin and I'm laughing inside, 'cause I've just realised that life was too short to be nasty....Now it's too late to be nice."

"Six weeks later I wakes up in the hospital...back from the dead, half paralysed. In a way, I suppose I was pretty lucky...

I'd only broken me left leg in three places, dislocated me hip and broke me jaw. It only hurt when I laughed, but I didin't mind that....

I laughed 'til I cried. An' I enjoyed the pain, 'cause for the first time in me life, I was glad to be alive. I lay there counting me blessings."

Tommy pointed to himself..."Me..." He said...

..."Aa was the luckiest bloody fella in the whole bloody world!!"

"Call that lucky...yer barmy owld bugger." I said

"Whey-aye..Geordie man, it could have been a lot worse.

I could have hit that water with me legs wide apart....it was like landing on concrete, me bollocks would have burst!!"

"Ouch!!" yelled Bella, even though she'd never have Bollocks, she still felt the pain.

Tommy took a long slurp from his pint and smacked his lips, rolling his eye's, he looked inside his head and remembered...

"The worst part..." He said staring into his pint and twisting up his face at the memory..."Was that dirty stinking water!!!...It's a good job they pumped my stomach, 'cause they reckon it's pure poison and nowt could live in that dirty rotten water!!"

"An' her, what happened to Her?...Surelly she came to see you in the hospital!!" Bella queried.

"Rosie??..."Says Tommy with feeling...."Didn't see head nor tail of her." Tommy then hesitated..."Naw...I tell a lie, I opens the *News Of The World*... and there she was staring at me, bold as brass – under a headline..

**"ARSE OWA BOLLOCKS I WENT....
AN' I SWEAR TO GOD THAT SHE WAS DRIVING..."**

...they meant me didn't they, and I had to laugh. Who the F*ck is daft
enough to fall off the Tyne Bridge....I bloody well jumped...didn't I!!"
"So...." Asked Bella, "Yer never set eye's on her again?"
"Aa' certainly did flower..." Tommy answered....
"Aa' was just outa hospital an' on the mend...felt glad to be alive I did. Aa
was nearly exploding with joy...well I felt bloody well immortal, but even
so, I made sure I looked both ways before crossin' the road....
That's when I saw her....Staring at me, with a look of madness in her eye's.
Then she gave me her Mona Lisa smile....a bit like a cat gives a mouse."
"Were was that then?" Bella queried.
"In Byker....she was with another fella, He looked a right spiv.
They were in his flashy motor car, an' he was smoking a greet big fat
cigar!!" Tommy ranted.
"A motor car?" said Bella, who loved posh cars, men with a lot of money
and she didn't even mind if he smoked big fat cigars..."What make of car
was it?" She queried....That was important to Bella.
Tommy rolled his eyes and looked inside her head for the memory.
"A Morris!!" He replied..."Aye, a bottle-green Morris Minor."
"Aye, a car...eh!!"...Old Frankie butted in...."Yer can't compete with a
motor car, especially a Morris Minor!!"
"Too bloody true!!" Tommy agreed snapping his fingers.

"Not in a bloody wheel-chair yer cannit!!" Tommy ranted....
..."The bastard only went an' run me over, still hangin' on to me crutches.
Arse owa Bollocks I went, only breaking me other bloody leg.....An' I
swear to God that she was driving!!"

Tommy limped away to the toilets for a slash and when he came back I
was almost certain he was limping on the other leg.

"An' the bairn..." Bella asked, "What about the bairn?"
"Huh...!" Say's Tommy....."It was only a bloody false alarm."
"Never in the world." Bella said..."So it was all for nowt then!!"
Tommy pondered before answering with laughter in his voice...
"Naw, I wouldn't say that....not really."
"An' how the hell do you make that out!!" I asked him.

Tommy wagged his finger as he replied...

"Well I never did learn tro fly...but by Christ when I hit the Water.....Aa sharp learnt to swim!!..

Now I'm never away from Shipley Street swimming pool...plays havoc with me athelete's foot like!!"

That got a great laugh and we laughed even louder when Old Frankie told Tommy..."Hev yer ever tried steepin' 'em in Epsom-salts?"

Then he pulls off a shoe and sock, lifting a big smelly foot in the air...

"Worked bloody wonders for mine!!" Said Frankie wiggling his toes in the air.

Tommy rolled his shoulders and took a deep breath relaxing before he spoke.. "Well that's all folks!!" ...mimicking a cartoon voice.

It was almost half eight, he'd been acting out the tale for two and a half hours...."I'll just finish this pint and I'll have to go."

He threw back his pint and took a deep swallow...Taking a gasp he then said.."Unless there's anything you'd like to know before I finally lay this ghost to rest?"

He seemed relieved to have finally got it off his chest.

I put me head on his shoulder and whispered in his ear.."Tommy, there is one thing I'd like to ask but you needn't tell us if it's a bit of a sore point!!"

"Naw!!" Replied Tommy, "Not at all, nowts the bother....fire away!!"

"Any regrets Tommy lad...any regrets??" I asked.

"No...no regrets...Let there be no, no reg-ret!!" Bella sang to Tommy in her best French accent as he drained his glass.

Tommy held the glass up to the light and stared through it as if it were a crystal ball.

The last dregs ran down the inside of the empty glass...before Tommy spoke.

"Regrets...?" He almost sang, then went silent...as did the whole bar.

"Gan on then...tell us!!" I shouted to remind him.

He replied loud and clear.."Oh aye, Geordie mate...I've a couple I suppose. Like she kept me Rolex watch, me medallion and me solid gold snake ring with blood-red ruby eyes!!"

A loud cheer went up and they gave Tommy a wonderful round of applause, it had been a great show...a night they'd never forget in years to come. They would all brag...

"Me, I was there the night Tommy-Owa- The Bridge telt his tale!!"

And, I've no doubt at all...Rosie will become more beautiful and
Tommy will grow
with time to be dashing, handsome and never missing his turn in the Bar.
It will be Bykers answer to Romeo and Juliet....an' I'll tell yer something
for
nowt....just as sure as God made born again Christians...Tommy will
become a
*Saint.....yes I can see it now..***Saint Tommy owa The Bridge"*** *– The*
Patron Saint
of Bridge Jumpers. He'll be stuck on a solid gold medallion and he'll have
wings an' a
snake for a halo...with Ruby red eyes.

Tommy's face glowed with pride, he was really milking it now.

He took a bow, his eyes lit up, he was playing out the role to the very end.

"Anyway..." He joked.."It's all Water under the Bridge!!"

That brought the house down...

"Water under the bloody bridge!!" Tommy repeated his punch line, bringing an end to the show.

"That the time??" Tommy asked, looking up at the clock in the Bar.

"It's ten minutes fast!!" I told him....The clock had always been ten minutes fast.

"Anyway, time for me to go...I'm away to the Salvation Army Hut down Byker Bank...Can yer believe it!!" He continued and nodded a righteous little nod...." 'Am gonna give a bit of a talk on the evils of drink."

"Aye!!" I told him..."That'll be the day!!"

Bella laughed and leaned over the counter telling him, "Yer must be joking!!" I agreed...."Yer rat-arsed!!"

"Look..." says Tommy.."It's gorra be done, there's nowt wrong with saving a few souls!!"

Bella laughed even louder this time..."Now diven't tell us your one of 'em born again Christians??"

She mocked, "A right pain in the bloody arse they are!!"

250

Bella had nothing against religion, until the night her waster of a husband had walked out on her and the kids to become a bible-basher.

Bloody Jehova Wittness's, it stuck in her throat.

"Naw!!" Says Tommy…

"Aa wouldn't gan that far. I'll admit I've seen the light alright, but I'm not blinded by it!!… To be honest, there's this lass there that fancies me rotten. She sings like an Angel and plays the trombone in The Sally-Army Band. Well you know me, I'm a bit shy like an' the drink helps loosen me tongue."

"Loosen???" Bella exclaimed.."If yer drink anymore, it'll jump right out of yer gob!!"

"Geordie!!" said Tommy, nudging me in the side with a bony elbow…"Just had a thought…would yer not fancy joinin' us in the band this Sunday, yer more than welcome!!"

It was awfully hard not to laugh…"Naw thanks Tommy Lad, but Thanks anyway!!" I replied.

Tommy was out to save souls, but this soul didn't want to be saved.

However, Tommy wasn't gonna give up with a fight…

"Gan on Geordie man, it's bloody well great, you'll love it!! …. Best thing I've ever done.…'am in me glory banging on that big base drum. Would yer fancy a go on the triangle for starters…if so, there's one gannin' beggin'… so there is!!"

It was awful hard to keep a straight face as I imagined myself marching down Shields Road pinging on me triangle..an' me supposed to be a bit of a hard case. I thought me Fatha would turn over in his grave.

"Naw thanks all the same Tommy but it was nice of you to ask mate."

"Nay botha mate." Say's Tommy…"It's nice to be nice." He added with a twinkle in his eye.

Now that gets me thinkin' to meself, ain't it strange how people change. When I was
a kid, I was mad at the world…I wanted to rip-up-tree's.
Now, I want to plant them.
It made you think, it really did make yer want to believe in God.

Tommy must have read me mind…"Geordie!!" He whispered in me ear …."Aa' really did see God,…y'knaa!!"

Yesterday I would have laughed…not today though…"Where??" I asked.

"When I lay spread-eagled on Shields Road!!!"

"Will yer give-owa man...How do you know it was God??" I blurted.
Tommy crossed himself..."Oh it was God alright...couldn't be any Bugger else....Well Could it??":
"What did he look like...this God??"

He paused then continued..."Aa' know it sounds daft but he was beautiful and I'm sure he was smiling at me."
"Sure it wasn't a laugh!!" I asked.
"Naw.." He said..."It was a smile alright...definitely a smile and when he he saw the state of me, he started to cry...Tears of sorrow for me!!"
"How'd yer know he was crying??" I questioned.
"Geordie man, I might have been laying on the road mangled..an' half dead, but even I could tell....It was pissing down with rain!!"

Tommy was waving his goobye's now, getting ready for the off...but he wasn't gonna go without having one last go at me...
"Geordie, now are yer sure yer wouldn't like to come along an' join us on Sunday??....I mean if it's the triangle yer worried about I'm nearly sure I could get yer a tambourine."
"Naw, I'm sure but thanks again.." I lied.
"Yer don't know what yer missin' man!!" Tommy preached.
"Tommy...."
"Aye...."
"I'd rather pull a Elephant out me arse!!" I responded sarcastically.
Tommy looked sad, he'd lost a soul and found an arse-hole!!!
"I'll tell yer what, I'll give you a wave from the bar window as you march past." I told him.
Tommy's eyes lit up..."Will yer now!!"
"Aa definitely will." I replied.
"We all will.." Yelled Bella and broadcast it to the crowd....
"Well won't we....!!" She demanded...

..."**We certainly will**!!" *A chorus of voices answered back.*

A tear came to Tommy's eye..." A'm really chuffed...that would be really nice." He said with a quiver in his voice....
"God bless you all....Live every day like it was yer last ... 'cause one day it will be....We should all learn to live in peace in this life or we will never **R**est **I**n **P**eace...in the next!!"

252

The tear ran down Tommy's cheek...as he turned to go, he hesitated...eye's sparkled and his face lit up..."I've just remembered that bloody song!!" He said...."that one from the pictures."....
He began to hum then burst into song...

"WHEN YOU WALK THROUGH A STORM...."

He sang with such feeling...without knowing, I'm humming along... Bella's wonderful voice comes in on....

"HOLD YOUR HEAD UP HIGH...."

Everyone in the bar is now singing...

"AND DON'T BE AFRAID OF THE DARK...."

And as if by magic, for the first time in days, the sun burst through heavy black clouds...flooding the bar in a golden glow.

Everyone are up on their feet now, singing their hearts out...
"...AND YOU'LL NEVER WALK ALONE..."

And there's this wonderful feeling....this bloody marvellous feeling runs through me body from the top of me head, to the tips of me toes.
I'm singing...I don't know why...'cause I don't sing.
A'm singing at the top of me voice....

"YOU'LL.....NE—V – V ER.....WALK....A—LO—NE!!!"

And sure enough everybody cried at the end...and the local lads don't cry easy.
Funny how sweet and sentimental music can make the hardest of 'cases cry.

....

However, they all more than made up for it come Sunday.

253

**EVERYONE LAUGHED 'TIL THEY CRIED..
WHEN TOMMY MARCHED PAST US,
BANGING ON HIS BIG BASS DRUM....**

Everyone laughed 'til they cried, when Tommy marched past us, as proud as punch...banging on his big bass drum...I'd never seen him as happy...he had hope in his heart and he'll never walk alone...
In The Salvation Army Band....that is – He'll never walk alone!!!

....

Like I say – Let them laugh....let them all laugh.
Nowt bothers Tommy anymore...'cause he knows for a fact that he's gonna
have the last laugh...When he's way up there..
Polishin' the stars....
Come The Glorious End.

....

THE END

And The Blossom Fell

"And The Blossom Fell."

I had to sort me rubbish out the other day.

Hah!! ... Wor Lass only threatened to leave us if I didn't get rid of most of that old junk I'd stashed under the bed – Her words...not mine!

Mind You, she's right an All, I'm tellin' Yer, I couldn't believe me eyes.

The story of my life was under that bed. The deeper I dug, the further back in time I went. I didn't find any Dinosaurs, but what I did find was me old treasure chest with a Skull an' Crossbones painted on the lid.................I couldn't wait to open it, so I did.

Army badges, marbles, sea shells, smooth bonny pebbles, a jack knife, one headless soldier, a Yellow faded Newspaper cutting an' bloody hell, I couldn't believe me eyes...me Owld Catta-Y!!

I had to laugh...My God that takes me way back.

Back to the time when I was a scared, mixed up kid who didn't know who I was or where I was goin'. So I had to keep tellin' mesel', "There's nowt really wrong with this life, is there? Well nowt that a bloody miracle couldn't put right...God help us!!":

And maybe he would, but it was up to me wasn't it....one way or another, I'd have to help meself!!

....

Me Fatha' was effin' an' blindin' as I made me escape down our back stairs.

"Just yee wait 'til 'Aa get's me hands on yer!!...Yer unlucky little swine!!"

Unlucky, because his horse *Lucky Lad*, had....unluckily fell at the first fence.

I've heard it said, "Life's a race, from the cradle to the grave." Well, if it is, I'll tell you somethin' for nowt, me...I wasn't gonna fall at the first hurdle.

Me Fatha' was my first hurdle, wasn't he...And probably the hardest I'd ever have to clear. So you could say, that if you could get over him, it would put me in good stead for Life's Race.

I suppose even at an early age I was a bit of a philosopher...wasn't I.

As I dived through the back door, he was still yellin'," Aa'll bloody well murder Yer!!"

Murder, because I'd put his bet on. Had to laugh though..i'd only went and changed his daft bet didn't I. Family Man..romped home at 6 to 1. Gave me Ma the winnings...well it was rightfully hers anyway.

Laughin' me head off, I yanked me braces up and with a hop-an'-a-skip I broke into a run. Sparks flew as me hob-nail boots clattered off the cobbles. Nearly got hit by a tram crossin' Shields road.
People yellin' somethin' or other as I headed towards Byker Bank, where I followed the Ouseburn without so much as breakin' me stride.
And the best bit...I didn't even have to think about it...Me feet knew the way.

Shafts of Sunlight formed warm pools of Yellow light in rich Green undergrowth, the air was full of bird Song.
The Sweet clean smell could have been a million Miles away from Bykers' belchin' chimneys and the soot-blackened back-to-back ram-shackled houses. Under a magnificent spreadin' Chestnut Tree, I lay on a Golden bed of leaves and gazed up in wonder at a tree enclosed sky and dreamed with my eyes wide open. I felt safe here...Never ever wanted to go back. It was always the hunger pang in me belly that forced me home...and back to reality.
Even so, I slept with a smile on me face and dreamt sweet dreams of Jesmond Dene.

....

In the grip of Winter, the sleeping giant formed a natural domed Cathedral.
Its far reaching branches black against a steely Winter Sky.
'Twas as Holy a setting as any man-made place of worship and definitely as close to heaven as I'd ever get...and probably a lot closer than most!!

....

Come Spring, massive knotted roots gripped Mother Natures' life-giving earth.
The Chestnut stirred....Brown furry buds swelled the burst.
Blossoms bloomed.

Hand-like leaves stretched and spread their green fingers...reaching, embracing the bluest of skies.

....

Summer came, bare footed I'd trod the surf of the forever ice-cold North Sea. Beach-combed the tidemark of the rippled shore.
Each and every handpicked polished pebble I weighed between finger & Thumb...before rolling gently between fingertips....testing for smoothness, shape and size.
Pockets bulging with smooth bonny pebbles I left a deeper footprint in Tynemouth's silver sands.

....

While back in the Dene, blossom fell like snow.
The faded...withered flowers turned to seed and with every sightin' the seed grew bigger.
How I willed those baby conkers to grow.
What a bloody marvellous feeling...life was sweet...when the blossom fell on me!!

Too thick...too thin..wrong shape...wrong size. Eagle eyed I scanned the Hawthorn hedgerows' branches.
Lop-sided...too big...too small..."Til Whoopee!!!". I'd spied the one.
It was definitely the right one.
Excited, but with great care I cut the perfect "Y".
Felt more than just pride as I gripped it tight in me fist. It sent a shiver down me spine. I was King Arthur, drawing the sword from the stone.

By Late Summer, young conkers hung in clusters. The warring elements took a heavy toll. Casualties of the battle lay strewn across the forest floor.

One eye closed, the other sighted along the edge of the narrow blade... with the skill of a surgeon, I ran Da's cut throat razor in a straight line, slicing through the rubber inner tube...as easy as cutting through Ma's paper thin spam!!
By early Autumn, the Chestnuts' casings really began to swell.

Still more fell before their time...still ripe. Soft green casings lay like open Oyster Shells, revealing an un-ripe pearl-white nut.

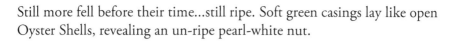

The Cobbler down our lane punched a couple of holes in the leather tongue I'd cut from one of Da's old work boots. Threading the inner tube elastic through the round neat holes. I then turned it back on itself and tied them together with twine. A Granny knot...me Granny herself would have been proud of.....followed by six half hitches.
I'd done it!!.....I'd finally lashed the elastic sling to the "Y"!!
I really did imagine I was Robin Hood with his Bow, the day I finally strung my Catapult.

Byker tip became my shooting range. Take careful aim....FIRE!!
Empty bottles or old tin can...anything became my target.
Could kill a rat at 30 Yards...a ball bearing between the eyes.
Dead-eye-Dick...Oh Aye, that was me.

By late Autumn, the Chestnut shell had changed colour to a motley-brown and swelled to gigantic proportions. It looked almost ready to explode... the countdown to the Conker season had begun!!

For the thousandth time me Fatha' threatened to kill us again!!
This time it was for the football pools. Can you believe it, the barmy old bugger only expected to win every week God sent.
He was an awful bad loser me Old Man!!

"This unlucky bloody hoose!!"...He'd start and throw his Pools coupon into the back of the fire. Like all bad losers, he'd look around for someone to blame. His eyes always stopped at me!
I suppose he couldn't help the way he was and I got used to his ways.
Even so, when he was home our house was like a mad house..I just had to get out. Especially since Today was the day of all days!!

Was smilin' when I jogged up our lane, had a pocket full of Tynemouth's finest pebbles. When I turned the corner I was laughin'. Had me Catapult in me back pocket...was headin' for the dene...life was great.

With a hop-an'-a-skip, I broke into a run. As I ran I felt happy inside. Thin grey clouds scurried across a laden Sky.

The fine touch of cool shadows gave me goose pimples as I entered the wood. Droplets of dew hung on every leaf. I squelched nature's carpet of sodden-leaves under hobnail boot.

Didn't seem real...I had to shake me head to un-scramble me brain. It wasn't a dream...it was much better...much better than any dream this!!

I whistled in wonder at the shear size of the Conker..high on the top most branch. For months I'd kept an agonising vigil, watchin' and waitin'... and waitin', willing it to grow. It was enormous...gigantic. The marvel was accomplished, it hung like a bomb, a spiked mine, ready to explode!!

I felt bloody marvellous, me heart was pumpin' with joy. It was more, much more than just a conker, it was my very own Excalibur and the Holy Grail plus Tolkiens' magic Ring all rolled into one.

All I needed now was a bit of luck, but then hadn't I made me own luck. But to be on the safe side, just for luck anyway, I spat three times and touched the livin' wood to ward off the evil eye!!....Evil eye..Hah!!

Primitive superstition sent a shiver down me spine and the stubble of me shaven head stood up like hair on a gooseberry. Me, superstitious...naw course I wasn't...well just a bit anyway!!

Slowly I drew back the loaded leather pouch.

At full stretch, I held the pull and studied the prize through the dead centre of the "Y". Closin' one eye, I took careful aim...time stood still.

Me heart was pumpin'...could feel the blood rushin' through me veins.

Back arched...legs astride, me toes gripped the sole of me boots, anchorin' me to the ground.

I could feel the power of the pull on the elastic..alive..it ran through finger and thumb and shot up my right arm!!

The left, was as straight and steady as Eros's statue holdin' his Bow. Couldn't miss. In me minds eye, I could already see it fall. Wouldn't miss. I focused me eye and held me breath...me heart skipped a beat, dead silence...I let fly!!!

Dares n't breath...in slow motion it came to Earth. With a muffled thump it hit the ground and bounced. "POP!!!" A small explosion burst the casin' apart. Rooted to the spot I looked on spellbound.
A huge heart-shaped....bloody-brown Conker landed at me feet.

Holdin' me prize in the palm of me hand, I could see me ugly mug grinnin' back at me..reflecting in the glistenin' polished new-born skin.
An' I'll swear to God, I could feel it's heart beat! .... But then again that might have been mine!!

Overnight, I found a hidden strength of mind as well as body, the like of which I'd only dreamed of. I wielded me Conker like Samson wielded the jawbone of an Ass. The battles were short and swift...always ending in the same way. Can you imagine the other kids eyes poppin' out and their mouths agape in disbelief, standin' with only their sad length of knotted string left danglin'. His Conker and pretender to the throne smashed to smithereens!! We were a great team...it took two to Conker.

Ninety sevens –a, ninety eights-a, I lost count after a Hundred!!
I almost felt immortal and I knew in me heart that me and the "King of all Conkers" would never be beaten. Big-headed ..Aye, I reckon I was an' all!! The men in our lane would bet on anything, they soon latched on to a sure thing. And I reckon me Fatha' must have won a small fortune. So for a short time at least, I'd became all the canny lads... Bloody Old Hypocrite...you had to laugh.

....

Our fame spread...Kids came from near and far...they couldn't believe their eyes.

"It's a billiard ball!!"..."It's a painted cannon ball!!"...They argued.
Had to show them it's empty shell-case, just to prove it.
One Kid still argued.."It came from outer-space!!"...You always get one!!

Had our picture in the local paper,.."Kid Conker"..The Headline..or was it "The Conker Kid". A local lad makes good. It would have made the front page if it hadn't been for that Hillary Fella..Conquerin' Everest!! But then again I suppose we were both "Conkerers" in our own way.

I ran out of opponents. Ended the Conker Season un-defeated.
Me, well I felt like the Heavyweight Boxin' Champion of the whole bloody world. For a short while, I became a bit of a hero...livin' the legend.

The livin' legend died with the changing' of the seasons and the hero faded away. Forgotten in time...that is until I sorted out me old rubbish last week!! Don't tell Wor Lass, but I'm goin' to hang on to me catapult. I could have cried when I dug me Conker out from the bottom of the box...a shadow of it's former self!!

Da' passed away some years ago. Hope he's gone to a better place.
I stopped hating him and learnt to laugh at him, another lifetime ago.
I remember that day as though it was yesterday.."Lucky Lad" fallin' at the first fence....It's sad, what a wasted life. All I ever wanted was for him to be proud of me, just like I was proud of him. Never mind, you live and learn.
Me...I vowed I'd be the opposite of me old fella, so in a way I'm grateful...I owe him....He helped make me what I am.

Took the Gran'bairn through the Dene, she'd never been before. Lovely day, the sun was shinin'..I'd forgotten how beautiful it was.

She's only five, you know what Bairns are like, couldn't shut her up.
She played touch an' cry, "Look, look Granda'!!" Pointin' to some small flower. She's great, her enthusiasm, she always wants to share with me. The bairn's a treasure; she's certainly given me a new lease of life.
Today, I told her we were on a secret mission.

As we stood in the shade of the giant Horse Chestnut, the memories came floodin' back.
"What is it Gran'Da'?" She asked, lookin at the shrivelled Chestnut I'd placed in her tiny hand.
"It's....er...it's a Conker, well a seed love."
"Is it dead, Gran'Da'...is it?" She whispered as she gently placed it in the ground.
"Naw pet, it's only asleep."
"Will it wake up...Gran'Da'...will it?" She replied.
"Only if yer wish hard enough, then it will."

"Will it grow, Gran'Da',...will it grow?" She asked all excited like.
"Why-Aye it will...but you've got to sing to it first pet!!"

And when Aa takes a good look at the bairn, she's a picture of good health and happiness...and thank God hers is a place where the Sun always shines. I suddenly realised how very precious life is and how it never really ends. Because we're at one with nature...The Seasons...of Life itself...part of all things...just as sure as the Bairn's part of me!!

And just t' prove it a voice of an Angel started singin'....

"All things bright and beautiful..."
A Skylark flew up...trillin' in harmony with her song...
"...All creatures great and small..."
Higher and higher it climbed...until it was just a song in the sky.
"...All things wise and wonderful..."

Me...cry..naw never.....well, course I bloody was.
"...The Lord God made us all."

At the end of the day, it's not what you come into this world with; it's what you bring into it.....And what you leave behind.

With a tear in my eye, I looked up into the canopy of this great Chestnut and just like all those years ago, Golden rays of sunlight shone through the green mosaic above us...and **the blossom fell**....just for us...**it fell!!!**

Wor Netty

By Mark James

"Goodbye Old Byker."

Oh...Old Bkyer...Where did she go??
That lovely Old Lady I knew so long ago.
Life was so simply way back then
Alas those days we can never live again.

To strangers you weren't a pretty sight
But to me you were the first love of my life
The canny folk that lived in those narrow streets
Brought you alive and made your heart beat.

The bairn's that ran barefoot through the cobbled lanes
Were the lifeblood that ran through your veins
It's folk not those old buildings that made you a place of worth
The Folk of Old Byker were the salt of the earth.

Alas, Old Byker you old love of mine
You grew too old and grey for these Modern Times.

They came and tore the heart and soul out of you
And built you up again all brand new
Now trees' and flowers grow in place of the cobbled lanes
A wall of houses brought you fame.

Oh how they changed your view
You're not the Old Girl I once knew
Good bye Old Girl...you Queen of the Tyne
The Girl I once loved in another time
Hello Young Lady...you look so fine
I could grow to love you...if only I had the time.

END OF

PART THREE

And The Blossom Fell

THE END

The Author...

Photo: Newcastle College

I was born in Byker, Newcastle upon Tyne in 1939.
Leaving school I could barely read or write.
At the age of 48 I attended Heaton Adult Education Centre...
The hardest part was picking up the pen.

33920458R00167

Printed in Poland
by Amazon Fulfillment
Poland Sp. z o.o., Wrocław